The Children's Guide

to

Parenting

Family Tales for Parents

by

Susie Reynolds Reece

The Children's Guide to Parenting

Family Tales for Parents

Dedication:

To my compassion, my humor,

and my fearlessness--

my three children,

you are my trio of strength,

joy and inspiration.

Table of Contents:

Prologue

All of the Family

Little House on the Parkway

The Children's Guide
to
Parenting
Family Tales for Parents

Prologue

About the Book:

While composing the CHILDREN'S GUIDE TO PARENTING, I planned on regaling readers with these wonderfully encompassing descriptions of my offspring-- illuminating both their beauty and their flaws-- effusively elaborating on my enduring love for them and offering my expansive knowledge and understanding of them as little kids and future grown-ups.

Then I thought, why not let them tell you? Who better to show us than the kids themselves, that kids are great, kids are funny, kids are crazy, kids can get away with things that adults can't--because they are kids. It's a big job to be a parent. So let laughter lead you through it.

The CHILDREN'S GUIDE TO PARENTING shows you how to maintain your sanity by coloring your perspective with 50 Shades of Humor.

Like the mountains of laundry endlessly rumbling about in the dryer because of your perpetually messy children, parenting is a like a mixed load of lights, darks, colors and delicates all thrown in at once tumbling about together. It is a world of mystery, mistakes, repetition, confusion, forgetfulness, chaos, joy, foul odors, repetition, hunger, happiness, laughter, hilarity, sadness, exhaustion, repetition, anger, forgiveness, tears, but more than anything, it is a world of love. Oh, and did I mention repetition?

All parents do their best and hope for some sort of sign or revelation to show us that we are doing everything perfectly. One of the first lessons our children teach us is that there is no such thing as perfection. My kids make sure I realize this hard fact repeatedly each and every day.

I am not able to achieve flawlessness because it does not truly exist. It plays poker with Sasquatch and the Loch Ness monster and rides on the backs of rainbow-adorned unicorns.

Kids will never allow us to achieve perfection, because they innately understand the reality of its non-existence so much better than we ever will. Simply put, they don't know what it means. As adults, we have forgotten this simple truth. Perfection is an unrealistic ideal that we humans created and continue to strive toward in order to keep us in pursuit of becoming new and improved versions of ourselves. This isn't bad until you start to feel badly about yourself because you are constantly striving for the unattainable, never to be satisfied. See, my kids taught me that! They taught me that perfection is nothing more than an illusion--an imaginary friend or foe.

We parents are here to not only love hard, but to laugh so hard we snort through our noses, realizing that kids have an unmatched knack for bringing us back to reality by showing us that 'perfect' is just another way of saying not good enough. Perfect is a fantasy. Kids are real.

The CHILDREN'S GUIDE TO PARENTING shows you something else that is real--there is no such thing as too much laughter (except maybe when it's out of control in church)-- and, it's a Godsend that kids give us countless comedic moments while we're raising them. Do you think we could possibly survive it otherwise?

I'll return shortly. I've got a mountain to climb (of dirty laundry that is).

The Children's Guide
to
Parenting

Family Tales for Parents

When to Expect the Unexpected

Have you fought with little people over bedtimes and meals? Have you found yourself pleading on your hands and knees for potty training success? Do you frequently resort to bribes or threats, even though you once swore you never would? Do you find yourself walking around searching for your phone-- while you are still talking on it? Do you wish your kids were born with an instruction manual in hand? Well then, THIS book can help. It will show you not only how to laugh in the face of the daunting task of parenting, but more importantly it will teach you to laugh at yourself while doing it!

The CHILDREN'S GUIDE TO PARENTING details what to expcct when you step into the adventure that is child rearing. Nothing is off limits here, simply because kids know no bounds. Becoming a successful parent is an acquired skill, like riding a bike. It's intimidating at first, but once you find your balance it becomes a skill you never forget. And that's a good thing, because parenting never really ends. Yes! I've heard rumors that some are still parenting when their 'little ones' are well into their 30's, 40's and 50's. If you are lucky, you become a grandparent ushering in a new generation of parents. By the way, grandchildren are the reward you get for raising your kids. Parenting probably stops around the time your kids are in their 60's, because by then, most parents are dead, but whatever. The point is, it's a lifelong skill, so take all the help you can get and learn it well.

Now, I know what you're thinking--how could I have paid so little for something worth so much? Don't be suspect of my generosity. While I am not an expert, I have been through it three times, and I am still going through it. My hope and intention is simply that my 'family tales,' experience, and friendly advice will spare you some of the growing pains of parenting. These words will help you hear, see, and perhaps even taste that you are not alone. Taste you ask? Well, we are dealing with kids here who live with all their senses, except common sense. So yes, you may very well taste the experience, too.

Let's face it; we parents are all just crazy, candy-covered zombies stumbling along hoping to trip on that rare recipe of how to raise well-adjusted, balanced nuggets of children in a world that spits out fewer of them every minute.

I have wished for an instruction manual to learn exactly what it is I need to do in order to raise my children the 'right' way. We all know the wrong ways to raise children because all too often new parents are told that their way is in fact, the wrong way. If there were a perfect parenting book, it would be so colossal; no one could lift it, let alone read it. Any book that came close to what I needed would probably be the A to Z Guide of how your children are nothing like anything in this book. Guess that explains why that elusive KIDS INSTRUCTION MANUAL has never come to be.

So, to recap: parenting is not about perfection. It is about compromise, duct tape, and realizing that sometimes you need to hide instead of seek. Both kids and adults teach through actions. We learn from our mistakes and we adjust so that we do not continue to make the same ones.

Sit and Stay Awhile

They say children are miracles. Children are our future. And, children are from the corn. (Wait a second strike that last one--sleep deprivation strikes again!) Where was I? Oh yeah. I am not sure who 'they' are because no one has responded to my Craigslist ad to claim this title yet. I will keep you posted on that front.

Anyway, supposedly children are little angels who flutter about and speak in classically tuned bell-like voices while reminding us every day how lucky we are that they have graced our lives with their presence. I have to admit, I don't feel that way all the time. In fact, I don't feel that way half of the time.

Most of my time is spent chasing (quite literally) half or fully naked, dirt smeared, hooligans who are using my _____ (Insert your item of choice here. No, really, try anything. It'll work, here try-- bra, marker, money, or even remote control; see what I mean? Fun, isn't it? In my case, it was glasses) as nose plugs while laughing frenetically at me as I run into things face first, while attempting to prevent said inserted item from becoming lodged in an orifice, resulting in an embarrassing Emergency Room visit.

I do my best to make it appear as though I have control over the situation and my little menaces. The truth is that they are the ones running things. It's been said that good and evil co-exist and my kids are living proof of it. They are just as much little devils as they are angels, but oh, they are cute! They're cuties "and they know it, know it, know it!"

And boy do they work it! How do they wield this power at such an innocent age??? Scary to think they are born with this natural ability to manipulate! Here's the game they play 'Let's see how far my cuteness will get me before she actually pulls out her own hair.' I just love that game, don't you?

The most important lesson my children have taught me is that humor will get you through the most challenging of times. It releases tension as the weight of problems drift away upon the sound of laughter. My parenting experiences have taught me that if I didn't laugh at myself, I might be the only silent one around.

Like millions of people, somehow, we ended up with three replicated, albeit tinier, versions of my husband and myself constantly circling us like bandits around covered wagons. I can't tell you exactly what we were thinking; perhaps it was that we weren't thinking at all. We are officially a Mom and Dad of three, with almost a decade of experience. It's shown us that our kids will teach us more about parenting than any parent ever could.

All of the Family
Welcome to Our World

My three children consume my every waking hour every single day along with all the candies that I have squirreled away in what I thought were well-hidden places. They terrorize one another in such calculating ways that I often question if I have given birth to child geniuses. The following is but a sampling of what their juvenile criminal minds are capable of conceiving:

- The youngest has already learned how to outmaneuver his older siblings in his ongoing attempt at world domination (it's a small world, but we don't have the heart to burst his bubble, but that's beside the point).

- While watching one child look frantically for an object, another child is not only sitting on it, but is suggesting bogus places to look for it.

- They have perfected the blame game to a point where I have to conclude that all three children were involved. Every single time!

Be afraid, be very afraid.

Each day I wake up to miniature hands grabbing me in unmentionable (this is a children's book after all) places. I find smiley-face stickers in crevices I didn't realize I had! After where they've been, their smiles seem to have turned to sly grins, wink, wink.

I am their indentured servant, a never-ending servitude that puts both joy and confusion on my face, slaps me around a bit at times, while also causing uncontrollable laughter bordering on hysteria. And I wouldn't change it for anything.

I've chosen a few of our favorite **Family Tales** to share with my fellow Moms and Dads to keep you smiling as you learn how to laugh your way through the unpredictable adventure of parenting. These sugar-dusted anecdotes are secretly covering healthy morsels of advice. Shhh. I won't tell if you don't.

I can't fully take credit for the majority of the lessons that lie within these stories because more often than not, I am (or my husband is in some cases) the humbled student of my child teachers who impart new knowledge daily. Allow me to introduce them and let the imparting begin!

My youngest, Mr. Alexander, aka The Grunt has proven us wrong on every parental front from the moment of his birth. You see, he was born grunting. Yes, you read correctly. Grunting. Not crying like almost every other newborn in the entire world, grunting. In fact, he has made me question his genetic makeup to the point where I have considered having him tested to see if he is the descendant of a long line of Hog Kings.

If Alexander wants it, he wants it now and grunts until he gets it. He is as stout as a bull and he refuses to be treated like a baby. If I lay him back in my arms to hold him, he will kick and swing like he is fighting for dear life. I can only imagine how dreadful nine months of being confined in my womb must have been for this little beast. Honestly, had I not seen him spring from me with my own eyes, I would have been easily convinced he was a half boy/half boar found in the wild. I shall dub him Alexander the Grunt, The Grunt for short.

My 'Malcom in the Middle' is Mr. Daevyn, aka Ding Ding. Yes, you read right (more on his name, and his catchy nickname, later). Daevyn is the epitome of the mischievous middle-child who will stop at nothing to garner attention. He runs into walls full steam ahead, fully intent on hitting his head before falling on his bum laughing so heartily that he breaks wind. This of course, only turbo-charges his laughter taking him to a level close to pure ecstasy/insanity.

His joy comes from the simple things, which he sees as wondrous and new. He is the secret-button pusher, the hider of candy and toys, the eater of dirt-- but not of dinner.

Finally, meet my oldest, Ms. Kenzie, or Kiki for short. She's the firstborn who immediately taught us how little we knew about caring for a child. We knew nothing (and I do mean NOTHING) about parenting. She is the princess who has force-fed us more than our share of foolish pre-parenting misconceptions (which we eventually spit out). She is the child who has suffered through our awkward 'practice' stage and somehow survived all the missteps we invariably took.

So, there you have the brain trust for this Mommy and Daddy. My hope is that our stories will inspire you to look at the lessons to be found in your own Family Tales. When asking questions, answers may be hidden, or even eaten, but you will find them if you seek them. The moral of the story is that you have what it takes to be a wonderful parent---you CAN do this--- you are just too grown-up to know it!

Are you ready for a tour through the life and times of our teachers? Their schedule is a <u>rigorous one</u>! I hope you can keep up!

BRB (Baby Rampage Beginning). Apparently, Godzilla has invaded my home. Let the battle begin. Enjoy!

Alexander the Grunt

What goes through a baby's mind all day long? I have interviewed my own baby and he grudgingly agreed to allow me to divulge his deepest, darkest desires and thoughts to the world. The contract was stringent. Apparently, I am indebted to him for 2 years of diapers, a vehicle, and college tuition to name but a few of his terms. However, his insight may just help us adults understand what goes on in the heads of tiny people.

Because he communicates through grunting, I will serve as his interpreter. Another duty to add to my ongoing servitude for his tiny highness.

Time to serve his mini-majesty's dinner, which he will most likely immediately throw on the floor. Off to find that indestructible silver platter.

Inside the Grunt

When I wake up, I'll need my diaper changed immediately. Don't use that powder stuff or I will try to eat it and any hands that may be attached to it. I expect you to have everything laid out, assembly line style, or I will wiggle my way to freedom. I may expect a clean diaper, but I will not allow your wrangling skills to get rusty.

While you're at it, go ahead and strip down the bed and clean it too, because for some reason I stink worse than any baby should. I would appreciate it if you would not verbalize my stench or I will be sure to cry out in protest of your belittling behavior. You will refer to all my odors as floral in essence from this moment forward.

Mom Prob: How to deal with an odiferous child while diaper changing.

a. Be sure to have all of your diapering supplies ready—the diaper, wipes, cream, lotion, powder, etc., laid out, open, and ready to go, so you can grab them quickly, while keeping one hand on baby as you diaper.
b. No matter how tempted or curious you may be, DO NOT breathe through your nose during this process. (My husband turns his shirt into a makeshift gas mask by pulling it up over his face as he does his diaper duty.)
c. Hold your breath and harness your inner speedster.
d. Feed your child an impeccably balanced diet of foods, so that there is no stench to avoid. (This

Now that we've got the diapering straight, I demand to be present while you wash my linens. I will oversee all duties that involve my hygiene and property. While you strip the crib sheets and load the washing machine, I will be judging you quietly. You have 2 minutes to do all of this, because I have already soiled my diaper again and I desperately need to take my bath--now!

All right, you've got about 20 minutes from the start of the bath before I require my breakfast. I would suggest you keep this time limit in mind while I'm basking in my own glory. Oh, how I love to sit in the porcelain bowl and let the waters of heaven rain down on me like the deity that I believe I am. Don't actually bathe me as I bask in my own glory, or you will face the wrath of Grunt like a hog on the hunt. When I give you the signal, a grunt of course, get me out of the tub, and I mean now, WOMAN!

Breakfast of Grunt-ions

If you have not fed me my breakfast by the time my tummy timer goes off, I expect to be placed gently in my walker. Once in the walker I will be running into the back of your heels because I know you love that feeling. You are allowed to make my brother's breakfast, but be quick about it. This little king waits for no one.

When I hear the blender, that will sound the alarm, and there is no turning it off until the food passes my lips. You know the drill--you must feed me as fast as super-humanly possible. If I don't think you're feeding me fast enough, I'll grunt with the force of a hurricane until I turn red with rage.

I expect my breakfast to be served at room temperature, no warmer, no colder. If it is not the exact temperature I desire, I shall not eat it! Any foods not meeting these requirements will be thrown back in the face of the server. I will take exactly two portions, and you will not pause in between, or be prepared for another harsh response. I see that learning is not your strong suit. I will tolerate it this time, but do not expect this leniency from me again.

After breakfast, I expect you to feed me a bottle, although I don't actually plan to drink it. I still want it and you will give it to me. Hold me while I look around lackadaisically in my food stupor. I'll touch your face sweetly a couple of times so you think you've done well. Then I'll smack you once to keep you in check. I am in charge, and don't you forget it, peasant!

It's all Fun and Grunts

So far so good. You can now let me play with all of my toys, and I do mean all of them! Get to finding them quickly. How is it that you are not better organized and prepared for this? Geeze, we go through this every day. Take note of my displeasure--with a grunt of disappointment, of course. Perhaps you need an apprentice to help keep your rubber ducks in a row.

Once you have finally found all of my favorite possessions, I will lie on my stomach and attack my toys for 20 minutes. They like it when I show them who is ruler. At this time, you are allowed to attend to my brother or perhaps you should stick around to gaze upon the sovereign one in action.

Ding-Ding

This is where things get interesting. Pay close attention, these boys don't willingly share their spotlight.

Ding-Ding is my never-ending fun machine. Like most 3-year-olds, his brain is bursting with ideas and creativity. He is a tangle of spider-webs (sans the spider), dinosaurs, superheroes and whatever else captures his imagination at any given moment.

Oh, to be young and full of energy. Clearly, he siphons it off me. I can almost feel the brio oozing out as I think about it. If 'two's company and three's a crowd,' then one 3-year-old is the equivalent of four crowds crammed into a pint sized mortal.

Mom Prob: Your kids have stuck straws in you and won't stop sucking until the last drop of you is gone.

Here's how I deal with this frequent and very serious Mom Prob.
a. Walk away from the situation. A few steps and some fresh air can dramatically change your attitude.
b. Call in the reinforcements. Enlist your in-laws, siblings, friends, etc.
c. Consider a Mom's day out to recharge because 'If Momma ain't happy, nobody's happy!' We all need time to recuperate and remember who we were before our former selves were swallowed up by caring for our kids.

d. Put them to bed a little earlier than usual and just stare at the wall. It may sound senseless, but it has saved me from going crazy on more than one occasion. The point is: schedule some 'you' time every day. Your survival AND your sanity depend on it!

Inside the Mind of Ding-Ding

Author's Note: If you are not yet familiar with *Three-enese*, a Translation Guide is provided on page 201 in the end of this book--because *his*-story is chock full of it.

The sun is almost up; it's time for me to wake everyone in the house. First, I must scavenge for any accidentally overlooked sweets. This has a twofold benefit: I get a full bellwy and I increase my energy efficiency before anyone else realizes what's hit them. I am a mastermind of eating goodies and not being caught. I'll just leave these candy wrappers in tiny inconspicuous piles around the house. I'm sure no one will notice. Seems like a great plan to me.

Now I need to wake up the crankiest member of the family. Hmm, decision time. I think the Grunt is my best option today. Mom always seems to like it when I wake him first. I'll just bust open his door and slam it against the wall as hard as possible. I am waking him up after all. Then to be certain he doesn't sleep through that, I will climb onto the slats of his crib, look down on him and scream, *"Wake up Ah-dander!"* That should do it. I've already accomplished so much this morning.

Once the Grunt is awake, I need to begin my morning aerobics. Only I have to figure out the best place to do it. My exercise involves a lot of rambunctious jumping and flailing of the arms accompanied by raucous vocal expression. I have found this to be the best cardio. It pumps me up, fueling an all-day energy high, which is just what I'm going for.

Hmmm. Where to do dis? I think I should do it in Mommy's bed. Her bed adds extra height to my jumps and increases my heart rate when I get close to the ceiling fan. I know she won't mind because she's asleep. I'll just crawl onto her bed. She won't even know I'm here. Hang on, lemme just pull myself up...aargh, nope that's the wrong place.

There is only one spot that I can manage to crawl up on. That was definitely not it. The rest of the bed is surrounded by towering mountains save for that elusive space. Aha, the best way up is right where she is lying. As I crawl over her face, I'll make sure to kick as hard as I can to keep that nefarious dragon (the one that lives under the bed) from ensnaring me. I'll keep Mommy sape from that evil creature.

Once I start my exercises, I'll jump as erratically as I can. That's the best way to get my cardio on. Thank goodness I ate all of that sugarcoated cereal right out of the box before anyone got up. Otherwise, I might not have had this extra energy to keep me going. I think robo-cardio is going to be my best option for now. *"I am a robot, I am a robot."* I yell this over and over, hoping it will drown out the sound of my crying brother. I am perfecting the sound of my speciously computer generated vocal chords needed for a feat of this Ultra Magnus-tude.

Oh, she moved...finally, the real fun has begun. She still isn't quite awake. I need to sit less than an inch from her face and bark like a cat until she finally wakes up. This woman just doesn't appreciate what a unique alarm clock I am. *"Meoark! Meoark! Mom. Mom. Mom. Meoark!"*

This seems to be working. I'm glad she's awake because I really need a playmate. *"Mom, mom, mom, I need eat, Mom."* She looks at me dazed for a second. I think I'll repeat myself just in case she didn't hear me. Five sounds like a good number; if only I knew how many actually make five. Oh well.

"Mom, Ah-dander is crying, Mom." That baby wakes up crying; maybe he needs candy, too. I'll remember that for tomorrow. *"Ding-Ding smart, Mom."*

As she is cleaning the Grunt and changing his sheets, I think dinosaurs should be running circles around her legs. Those dinosaurs are always trying to catch their tails. I smell Grunts diaper. *"Mom, dinosaur poo-poo is ahhhsome! Roaaaarrrr."*

Oh no, I am losing control of my feet, I think I'm going to.... *"Wahhhhh.... Mommy, I fall down!"* I can't stop crying until she acknowledges that I have collapsed under the weight of my dinosaur body. She has to pick me up and hold me before I will be okay again. There are specific steps that must be followed to properly console this boy. As soon as she has soothed my woes, I will laugh and jump out of her arms. This is how she knows that my tragic misfortune is all fixed up. *"I otay Mom. I tay now."*

I hear the bath water running! I can't ignore the call of the water. It cries to me like a Siren's song. *"Mom, I want take a bath with Ah-dander."* Even though she said, "No," I am still going to jump in the water. Once I am in, she can't do anything. Of course, I will need her to help me get my wet underwear off after we realize that I am going swimming anyway.

"Mom, I wet." She's probably going to go into her speech about how she told me no, but I don't listen unless my voice is involved. I have a nice voice. I like the way it sounds. It makes me happy. I can just make up whatever I want and it's the coolest thing I've ever heard. Just listen, *"Goaoaehoaydesasdf. I funny, Mom."*

We are one giant octopus. We have eight tentacles and they splash water all over the world. *"Wawee everywhere!!! Ahh, no don't spash me, no!! I spash you face. Aargh!"* I am the neatest octopus ever.

I love the cartoon-like face she makes when I get her wet and she has to change her clothes. The best is when I can get Ah-dander to spash her too. We are the aquatic duo. It's so much fun, until she turns the water off. That's the worst.

I can't play in the water-filled tub unless the water is actually running. I don't know why she hasn't learned this yet. I'll just whine and try to convince her that she needs to keep it on even if it starts spilling out. That only helps me play better. *"Mom, don't turn wawee off!"*

<u>**Mom Prob:**</u> Managing bath time messes.

a. Goggles come in handy when you are battling a bath time octopus, a.k.a. two in the tub.
b. Keep electronics out of the bathroom, or your child and your phone are both at risk of being submerged.
c. If you must get a photo of your bubble covered babies do so quickly.
d. When you have kids, it's essential to invest in a waterproof case. You'll thank me later.

Eenie, Meenie, My Name, Moe

By now you must be been wondering how Ding-Ding got his nickname. Well, here's the scoop.

Mama and Dada are the easiest sounds for a baby who is learning to speak, especially when it comes to grandparents' names. I remember the difficult decision-making process of helping my Mother-in-Law choose her name. We mulled over grannies, nanas, mamaws, and so on. Finally after weeks of thought, we made the epic decision that named her for the third time in her life.

She was to be the all-loving Nini, the giver of snacks and hugs, the saver from spankings -real or imaginary. In the end, we made a good choice because her name is an easy one to say. Children have a way of contorting names into something all their own, and that something is not always something good.

Parents tend to name everything for the sake of their children. We change everyday things to what we think sounds kid-friendly. It may seem like a silly habit, but it has stood the test of time.

Try saying, "Let's go potty," to a 29 year old buddy and watch what happens. How about, "The choo-choo was late picking me up today." Your boss is sure to excuse you for that one. Next time you're out try, "I'd like another bobble of beer, bartender." Instead of another beer, you'll likely be cut off. In parenting, most everything is nicknamed in baby talk.

The process of naming our first son was a real test for our marriage. His name came from an evolution of want, negotiation, and fear. Lots of fear. You see, for years I had wanted to name my firstborn son after my father, David.

My husband on the other hand, felt David was too common a name. He was rooting (and not silently I might add) to name our son after the Russian Composer Rachmaninoff (Rock-Mon-Ni-Noff). Something told me, and quite loudly I might add, that Rachmaninoff would be a very difficult name for a child to read, write, say, and let's face it, live up to.

So my husband concocted a distinctive name all our own – Daevyn. I got to name him after my father and he got to feel like a celebrity when we explained how to spell the child's name to everyone who asked--and everyone does!

When it comes time to actually say the name Daevyn responds to, it is nothing like the hybrid we created specifically for him. His chic name devolved into something primal as soon as the kid started to talk. So much for all that effort, creativity, and compromise.

Here's how it happened. During diaper changes, we thoroughly cleaned Daevyn's 'ding-ding' because no one wants a dirty ding-ding. It was a commonplace term in our household. "Hey boy, where is your diaper? You can't run around the house with your ding-ding hanging out."

He would wake me up in the morning, jumping on my bed naked, shaking his wee dinger all over the place laughing like a little madman. Boys seem to be born proud of their built-in 'toy.' Had he not been a 2-year-old, I might have called the police on him. No, I *would* have called, the moment I was awake enough to grasp the obscene situation.

Ding Ding Ding! You guessed it! Our son chose to rename himself his prized body part, which we obviously mentioned a few times too many. I have a Ding-Ding in my house, who happens to have a ding-ding of his very own.

Mom Prob: How not to laugh in the face of and reinforce 'bad' behavior?

As you have probably gathered by now, Rule #1 in the CHILDREN'S GUIDE TO PARENTING is to have (and maintain) a sense of humor while coping with the challenges of parenthood in order to survive it. However, there are times when kids innocently, and sometimes not so innocently, do and say things that elicit a belly laugh from the bigger people. At times like these, parents are faced with making the split-second decision of whether it will hurt or help for their child to see them burst out in laughter.

Here's my friendly advice for evaluating such situations:
a. Turn away! Diverting your eyes from the

laughter-invoking situation can help you realize you have to stay in parent mode. It also keeps the child from seeing that they have already weakened your stance.
b. *Realize that sometimes you just need to regain your composure. Take a moment if it is an issue that doesn't require an immediate response. Then calmly explain why the behavior was not acceptable. Let your kids know that although it was necessary for the behavior to be curbed, you still found it funny. It reinforces the notion that there is fun in improvement.*
c. *Breathe deeply and count to ten. Take a spa moment in your head, rejuvenate, relax, and resume parenting.*

The fun doesn't stop there. Take a trip with us to the local grocery store. Here I am with three children just trying to make it through the store as quickly as motherly possible. The whole time I am quietly in fear of a public display of private body parts. Mr. Mischief likes to shake things up whenever he can.

We reach the dairy section without incident and DD begins to yell at the top of his lungs, "Ding-Ding, Ding-Ding!" Children like to refer to themselves in third person, which only escalates their amusement during times like these. But this situation could become serious because his nickname shouted out loud is more times than not followed by a proud display of his 'little boy business.' With the alarm sounded, I could feel panic set in.

Before I could react, it began again! "Ding, Ding"....only this time, and much to my relief, it was followed by, "Ding, Ding wants eggs!" (Yes. Don't they all?) As all eyes stare at us, I quell his cries with a dozen large and swiftly slip out of the refrigerated section, Ninja skills activated.

Here's another example of nicknames gone wild. Once as I was attempting to change the boy, he ran off and stood stripped down in front of his reflection on the oven door. He began to 'shake it like a Polaroid picture' yelling, "Ding-Ding shake his ding-ding" repeatedly until he couldn't help but laugh and say, "I funny." Well, he wasn't wrong.

Churches and weddings also prove to be irresistible places for Ding-Ding to showcase his extreme pride in his appendage. Remind your kids to choose their nicknames wisely because one of these days when they will be called by it with an adult voice and may no longer like how that cute nickname sounds.

Taste Like Eggs

Now that you've solved the riddle of Ding-Ding, let's get back to the kid grind.

Well, that didn't work. *"Mom, I need eat. I want get out"* I still don't understand why I can't run around nakey. It seems like everything would be so much easier if I could. When she tries to put my shirt over my head I will try to stick my foot in like it's a sneaky snake. " 'Prise Mom, my foot is in the hole!" I don't know why she doesn't appreciate the humor of this.

Oh well. After she determines the correct positioning of this required clothing, I can finally get some food. She moves slowly, but I'll cut her a little slack. She didn't have any of my secret-weapon super-candy. She finally gets to the kitchen and opens the magic box. I love that box. The foods live in there. She calls it the refrigerator, but I know it's a magic box that makes food just for me.

Finally, it's time for the choices. She's always asking me to pick between two things. Even though I'm going to tell her I want one; I'm really going to eat both. Watch how I do dis.

She has to make food for me and my brother. Then she will cook for herself. Before she gets done making my brother's food I'll have eaten all of my food. Then I will politely place my request in a way that guarantees she will make me some eggs.

"Mom, make me some eggs. I eat my foods. I want eggs." We end up having a short debate, but I will win. She might as well just make me all the eggs, but as long as I get some I guess it doesn't matter. It would be much easier my way though.

Wow, these eggs taste like--eggs. I don't think I can eat all of them. I believe I will just have two bites. Then I'll throw the rest on the table and floor so it looks like I ate it all. It's probably best if it appears to be an accident. As I throw them down I will yell out, *"oops"* just to make it look legit. *"Mom, I done, Mom. I want get down."*

I'll run from woom to woom driving my matchbox cars all over the walls, table, and mirrors while she cleans the kitchen. *"Awoooooooooo!!!"*

GRUNT-erupting Again

Now, you have given your other son enough attention, so I will crawl over to you like a lion stalking its prey. Once I reach you, I will make certain you understand your rightful place in my kingdom. Hold me for 15 minutes while I cry for no apparent reason. I am just letting you know exactly what I think of your behavior. Thank you. That was satisfactory.

All right, I will now finish the bottle I didn't want earlier. Bring it to me this instant! Make sure you don't have an attitude about it either, wench! Once I drink all I can stomach, I'll spill the remaining milk on your head. I *won't* cry over it.

Now it is my playtime again. I will be occupied for about 30 minutes. Do not disturb me, as I have important work to do. If you begin to look as though your schedule is light, I will instantly make more demands on you. In fact, if you begin to look like a crazed monkey jumping off walls or as you call it 'cleaning' I will extract more from you. I may just make more demands for no reason at all. This will teach you the wisdom of always being prepared. You'll thank me one day.

It is time for you to take me to my crib for a nap. My bed had better be cleaned and properly prepared by now. I strongly suggest you remove all noise producing toys (especially the ones that sound as though they are having the life choked out of them) so they do not wake me mid-way through my nap. While you are at it, invest in some batteries to save those toys from dying a slow and agonizing death.

<u>**Mom Prob:**</u> Keeping up with the batteries.

In a world of electronic toys, what's a mother to do? Could they make it any more inconvenient to change batteries? I mean really. Is it any wonder we live in a disposable society? "Ain't nobody got time for that!" If you, like me, prefer to get the most out of your investment, here are a couple suggestions.
a. At the time of purchase buy an extra set(s) of batteries and keep said batteries together in the same safe place as the extra tiny screwdriver, you know, the only one that will open the battery compartment that's harder to get into than the toilet with a child lock on it.
b. If you are a ridiculously organized parent (a rare breed for sure), make a point of buying electronic devices that use the same size batteries, but the other rule still applies.

Ok, woman, In case you haven't figured it out, I don't actually want to sleep, so I will scream at you for about 5-10 minutes until I exhaust myself and realize that I DO in fact want to sleep. I will see you again in 30 minutes. Enjoy your fleeting free time, while it lasts.

While I am taking in my beauty rest, you should have: eaten lunch, cleaned the house, finished the laundry, and completed whatever 'work' it is you have to do. If you need to tend to my brother, then add that to the list as well. I strongly suggest that you tiptoe about the house as if you were a ballerina. Otherwise, I will wake with a vengeance! This is my way of cultivating your innate dancing skills. You'll thank your benevolent leader later.

State-DING the Obvious

Here comes Ding-Ding with his opinion once again.

In a minute, she's going to give the Grunt a bottle. As soon as she sits down, I am going to need to save myself from the lava floor. The only sape rock on the island is the one she is sitting on. I guess I am just going to have to crawl onto it with her and my brother. Maybe if I squeeze I can make enough room.

"Ergh, ah, I need climb up. Ah-dander, moob ober. Dank-coo, Ah-dander." This is much better. If I push my knees into her stomach a little more then I will feel nice and cozy. You can't get me now hot lava! *"Ha, ha, ha!!!"*

Ah-dander takes forever to drink his bottle. Hurry up so I can wrestle with Mommy. I'm the Power Ranger transformee and she is the bad guy. The transformee always beats the bad guy. *"I transformee! Go, go power rangers. Weeooo. Weeooo. Weeooo. Mom, I be fiderman now. You be black fiderman. Black fiderman is mean. You can't captch me Mom."* Spiderman wins again!

Sometimes when we wrestle I will laugh really hard. If my bellwy gets squished it makes me poo-poo burp. Mom tells me to say excuse me. She's so silly. *"No Mom. It not a burp. I not say scuse me. It a poo-poo burp."* Why doesn't she get it? It's okay though, cuz I smart.

While we are playing on the floor, the Grunt comes up and tries to get in between us. I found this cool plastic rope with lines and numbers on it. Mommy sometimes uses it to touch the wall when she's holding up pictures. I know what we should do. *"Mom, let's rope him and tie him dis."*

I'll hold it up so she can see my plan. She obviously has decided against it. I don't see how giving him a toy is better, but I guess I'll allow it. I'll hide that shiny flat rope for another time. Ah-dander may need to be hog-tied later, since he grunts like one.

DING-nado

She's started cleaning again. This is my cue to trash another room. That's what happens when you are caught in a tornado and are the only survivor. They simply come out of nowhere leaving a trail of devastation that gets Mommy mad. I am a lucky boy. Countless times I have been the only one left standing in the aftermath.

Oh, look, my car. Where did that come from? The tornado must have thrown it over there. Time for me to take this car on the road! I should probably see all the sights that are still intact before another tornado tears through here.

"Wegi and Mario will sabe da princess get in the car! I am their yellow marshmallow friend. You can't jump on me Koopa monster. Ding-Ding the yellow marshmallow. Marshamallow. Mmm. Candy. Where

can I get da candies? Candies I choose you! Where are they? Pikachu I choose you get me da candies. Mom, oohohoohoh yea Wheeooo. Wheeooo. Mmmmmhmmm. Umhumhumum. I dribe da cars and sabe da candies for my bellwy." Mommy doesn't hear when the tornadoes are coming. It's a good thing I have all these superhero friends to help me keep her safe.

I smell something. I think she is making food. I am hungry. She better be cooking something I like. She is always making me eat yucky food. *"Mom, whatchoo doing? You cookin' rice?"*

I jump around her hoping she will make me some rice. I love rice. White rice is squishy and sticky in my fingers. It's the best! No rice, no eat. I will hunger strike! Yea!

"Yay, Rice!" I have to touch it! I don't need a fork or spoon. It will only slow me down. Does Cookie Monster use a spoon? No! I am a rice-eating monster and I needs to shove all the rice in my mouth at once and eat it all. When I am done, there will be sticky flecks on the floor, walls, and ceiling. I am going to be a rice covered Ding-Ding roll. No need for other foods. A pound of rice is perfect to fill my tummy.

When the Grunt wakes up, Mommy will do her silly voices for him. I love her funny voices. I think I will be a frog today. *"Ribbit, ribbit."* Ah-dander is going to love me being a frog. Maybe I can even help

Mommy get him to laugh. *"Ah-dander laugh! Ribbit."* If that doesn't work then I'll just jump over him since he is small and I am big. *"Ribbit."* Otay, I just crawl over him. He won't sit still so I can jump. *"No, Ah-dander, I a frog. You sit dere and I jumper higher."* I win.

Wait, I think Mommy is about to start walking around with Grunt. I think I'll tag along for a ride too. She won't mind if I grab onto her legs. She won't even notice I'm there. *"Mom, go fast! Faster."*

Slowing DINGs Down

While you give Ah-dander a bottle you need to pay attention to me too. *"Mom, I a baby, too. Hold me like a baby."* I'll just look at her with my puppy dog eyes and she will have to pick me up. Ah-dander is going to try and push me so I'll sit on top of him. He always tries to kick me out of Mommy's lap.

Maybe I can sit on her chest while he sits in her lap. Let me see if there is enough room. Hold on, squeeze in there, just a little more. Move her head out of the way. Yea, that's good. I'll just stay here under her chin.

I hear the doorknob. *"Kiki home from school!!! Weeeeeee!"* As she tries to do her homework, I am going to run in and out of the kitchen every five seconds until she is done. Maybe I should climb in between the table and chairs and crawl over her lap too. This is where those jumping skills really come into play.

"Mom, Kiki do her homeworks. I help, Mom." Kiki needs to hurry up and play with me. I need to show her tornado. Homeworks is no fun. Finally, she's done. *"Kiki, let's play."* I can't wait to wrestle in the pile of toys with Kiki.

I am the biggerest and I am going to jump off the mountain of toys onto her head. That sounds like a brilliant idea to me! *"Watch out Kiki, here I come! Wheeeeeee- aaaaaaaaaa! MOM! I got hurt."*

After a replay of My Consolation: Part 2 I think I'll will settle down. Then again I may not. I should go play with all the toys in Grunt's room. Maybe I should bring them to him in the living room. Better yet, I will just hide them all over the house, so he can have them no matter what room he is in. I am genius.

Now that I'm done, I'll give Mommy a big hug. *"I duba you Mommy."*

Mom Prob: *What to do with boo-boos.*

a. First and foremost, DON'T react before your child does! Your ooos, owwws and poor babies will only serve to accelerate their emotional intensity.
b. Evaluate the seriousness of the situation.
c. Listen and distinguish. Babies and toddlers have different cries for different situations. If they are truly in pain, you will know to get

them the care they need.

d. When a minor accident is creating major attention, most often the child simply wants to know that you are concerned and needs assurance that everything is all right. Neon Band-Aids work like magic in these moments, especially when sealed with a kiss.

Meet Kiki

Finally, it's time for the oldest to interject a little knowledge.

Even though they are both tiny human beings, girls are an entirely different species from boys. They couldn't be more different from one another, and not just anatomically. Girls live in a world all their own. My daughter was fortunate enough to be born into the 'girl club,' but she is also a proud member of the firstborn club, a sub-species. It may sound alluring, but the first-born club is not all that.

Think about it, the oldest child is the one on whom parents perform their trial and error child-rearing experiments. Also known as the 'practice kid,' they are the unfortunate ones who must endure the most serious, harsh and rigid versions of their parents. By the time, parents get to kid number three you find that they just don't have the same commitment to, or energy for strictness (or even getting out of bed like they once did). The innocent girl never knew what she was getting herself into by being born first. She's now 9 years old, almost a Tween (in between single digits and teen numbers in age). She believes she has the mind of a 30 year old, when really she has virtually no life experience.

I look in the mirror every morning and do my best to travel back in time to recall what it was like to be 9, to help me better understand my girl. I should easily remember the inner-workings of being a young girl; after all, it wasn't very long ago that I was her age, right?

Kiki's always been overflowing with innocence, most of the time. Case in point:

Kiki and the Cake

My best friend was about to have her second child. I excitedly volunteered to throw her a baby shower. I was eager to be the one to get everything together for her. I picked out the decorations. I organized all the activities. I planned the entire event but nothing was as important to me as her cake, the centerpiece around which everything was to revolve. Everyone knows that half of the success of a party is what you eat, particularly when there is a pregnant woman involved.

This cake had to be super special. Visions of baby booties (instead of sugar plums) swirled in my head. I agonized over it for several days and even fell asleep at night surrounded by my cake magazines, until one glorious morning I woke up to find my dream design. There it was the sweetest of images; the most exquisite three-tiered, pale turquoise cake. It was adorned with a handmade, edible, crescent shaped bassinet that had been delicately placed on top of the highest layer of fondant. As if that wasn't enough, it was surrounded by twinkling star candies and buttercream baby booties. It was THE consummate cake.

I proudly placed my order, taking care to handle all the cake business while my daughter was out of earshot. I knew that having a cake in the house with a terribly-2-year-old child was risky.

Now all I had to do was go and pick it up the day before the shower. I decided that I would secure it as late as possible the night before, to reduce the minimum time I would worry about it. Devising a plan to keep it a complete mystery from Kiki, I enlisted the help of my husband. He would occupy her while I channeled my best 007 to get the goods into our house undetected. I was quite proud of myself that I avoided her asking me what I was concealing under my cloak. Daddy done good! Everything was going smoothly.

I slid the cake as far back as possible in the corner of the counter and covered the box in an aluminum foil tent disguising it as leftovers so as not to signal a sweet seeking child's interest. I even got down on my knees to beg that the cake makes it to the...just kidding...to see what it would look like from a 2-year-old's point of view. All I could see from what would be her point of view was just a box corner with aluminum on it. Nothing to see here. Furthermore, it was high enough that she would have great difficulty reaching it, being only 31 inches tall.

It was time for me to tuck in my little bed-bug for the night anyway. This covert confection operation was coming down to the wire. All I had to do was make it through the night. I would be up first thing in the morning, with an eagle eye on that cake. Excited and relieved I went to bed. I just couldn't wait to present this mouthwatering masterpiece.

That cake's survival kept me up most of the night. The next morning I rolled out of bed and crept downstairs. I peeked at the counter. Everything was still in place. I sighed with relief that the cake had made it through the night in one piece, so there would be plenty of pieces for the pregnancy celebrating partygoers to enjoy.

I spent the morning happily preparing for the afternoon's event, creating all sorts of finger foods, the excess of which was found by tiny, tubby, little fingers. She was so happy stuffing all sorts of fun foods in her face. I smiled lovingly and thought, 'Such a little angel. I will have to save her a big piece of that secret cake and surprise it with her later.' But the surprise was on me.

I began packing up. The last thing to do was to transfer the cake to a decorative platter. I opened the box and peeled back the aluminum foil unveiling half of what was once an elaborate cake creation. The other half had been stripped naked. My daughter devoured as much of it as her little belly could stomach, as evidenced by the missing fondant and the huge bite in the shape of her mouth, with tiny finger holes surrounding it!

Kiki must have pulled the chair over, climbed onto the counter and face planted into that cake! And without missing a beat, she replaced the foil to 'foil' her crime-- without leaving so much as a crumb or a smudge of frosting!

It was a hard lesson to learn about how cunning kids can be, even the sweet, 'innocent' ones!

Mom Prob: Kids are climbers at an early age.

It's part of their exploration phase. They learn where all of the 'fun' things or snacks live by watching you. Eventually, children will find a way into a sticky situation, whether you are looking or not. Being aware of where your children are and setting boundaries is key to heading this off at the pass. Keep dangerous products locked up tight, out of sight and out of reach of those curious little hands. Remember, they'll be watching 'every move you make.'

I was astonished. I was embarrassed. I was dazzled by the determination it took for her to pull off this stunt, right under my nose. Who would have thought a 2-year-old could conceive of such a calculating scheme, let alone have the agility to execute it undetected? Impressive skills, young one. Future spy in the making, no doubt.

I assumed that since the cake was just as I left it the night before, she wasn't even aware it was there. She somehow knew that as long as she left it exactly as she found it, I wouldn't know it had been touched. We were both right.

The party was a hit despite my dilapidated, half-eaten, two-faced cake. Shades of things to come for an expectant mother. You know, kinda like this book...

Grunt Force, Mama

When I wake furiously, I once again require your full attention. It's time for you to pick me up and hold me again for 20 minutes since I was forced against my will to take a nap. Prove to me that I should forgive you. I will wrestle with you just to remind you that I am a force to be reckoned with. In case you have forgotten, I AM THE WIGGLE MASTER. Please refer to diaper changes to refresh your memory.

Once you have calmed me down, you must play with me. This entails you talking to me in the goofy voice. Not that one, the other one, yes, that one. As you do this, I will first look at you like you are a lunatic. My eyes will widen with curiosity as my mouth hangs open and I drool in awe of your ridiculousness. I may tilt my head slightly, but don't take that as a sign that I am truly interested, because I am not. My attention span is waning.

After a few minutes, I will smile just enough to make you think that you are amusing me. I will not ever actually laugh at your pathetic performance, because, let's face it, you are just not that funny.

Continue attempting to entertain, me even though it's obvious I don't care. As you run through all of your tricks, I will make sure you know which ones displease me and will need to be cut from future acts.

Get down on the floor with me and show me how foolish you really are. Crawl on your belly as I look on at you in utter astonishment. I cannot believe that a grown woman would act like this! Where's the Baby Cam when I need it?

I love it when you act like you can't stand up again. The noises you make while you grab at your lower back are the best. I'll just sit and laugh as you pretend to cry. That is by far the funniest thing you do. That bit kills me.

Let's see, what else you've got? Throwing me in the air twice is good. No more than that, or I will cry from abject terror because I strongly suspect you must have dropped my brother on his head at some point. Otherwise, how do you explain his bizarre behavior? I've seen him stick his entire foot in his mouth, boot included. What's that all about?

Let me eat my toys on my play mat again for 20 more minutes. They need to be taught a lesson. I also have to deposit of some of this excess saliva. What better way to do that than by slobbering all over everything you will eventually touch? Don't ever say I didn't give you anything.

I'm going to stare at my brother while he dances about like a loon in his underwear. That kid is a mess. I wonder about you both sometimes. I see where he gets it though.

Where have you gone? I don't see you within our allotted two-foot perimeter. I will yell uncontrollably to make sure you have not left. Once you return to your designated area, I will be fine. Phew. That was close. I am warning you. Do not enrage the little King!

I may have to invest in one of those house arrest ankle bracelets for you. Maybe I will invent the first ever Mom-O-Meter to measure the acceptable distance a mother is allowed to step away and alerts the child if the boundary has been over-stepped. Good idea... ah, but my time is valuable. I think I'll just continue to drool and cry instead.

I require that you walk around holding me so that I can see things from a giant's perspective. Just to add a little excitement to your life, I will grab at your face and try to knock your glasses off. Don't move my hand or I will pull your hair like the reigns of a horse, because that's what you are to me. And I am the beast master!

Once I get those silly glasses in my hand I will throw them to the floor and laugh in your squinty face. What better way to remind you who has all the power? As you crawl on all fours like a blind sloth that has fallen from its tree, I will lie in wait. None shall wear glasses in my presence. Any who dares, shall face my wrath of destruction!

Ding-Ding looks through Mommy's glasses a little differently: Oh, her glasses fell on the floor. I think I should jump on them. I better be fast before she picks them up. It tay Mom, I'll clean them off for you. Maybe I should lick both sides to be sure they are really clean.

What's Taking You So Long?

After you have found those useless spectacles, you are to resume walking me around. Carry me, but do not dare to treat me like a baby. This means no kissing or hugging on me. You will work like the caretaker I have chosen you to be. Walk slowly and let me take in all of the sights.

Wait a second. What was that? I liked the face in the mirror. Go back. Let me stare at that gorgeous boy for a few more minutes. Who is that handsome lad? I like him. He even moves the same way I do. Wow. Okay, this is boring. I demand sustenance once again.

Feed me my bottle while I smack my legs as hard as I can. This is how I show you that you are far too slow. The loud slap of skin on skin is like a drum march. I will guzzle in unison with it.

Always the copycat, I know you think you have rhythm, but it would be best if you don't try to mimic me. Hurry woman, this belly isn't going to fill itself. Who taught you how to feed a monarch a bottle anyway?

Ah, yes that's the stuff right there. Now, I will chug all but the last 1/4 of the bottle and then I will chew on the nipple, as you try to figure out if I am done or not. No, I am NOT done. Kindly remove your hand from my bottle. I will make sure that you know you had better not take my bottle. Nice try you silly, silly woman.

Honey, I'm Home - From the Grunt's POV

I can tell that it's getting close to time for the bearded one to make his appearance so I am going to become fussier since you look nothing like him and I long to look upon his furry face. Things are about to change. This pushing me around (in a stroller) must stop! The bristled one is coming and your time is running out.

Dance for me; do your best to please me before it's too late. I don't want any more bottles or food but I'll still let you run about trying to track them down and present them to me as my royal gifts. I know your life is only fulfilled when you bring me things I don't really want. Why else would you constantly do it? I only do my best to make you happy.

You can try holding me as I do my babysaults. You know those baby somersaults that you enjoy so much. These are the most acrobatic of all the baby dances, kind of like monkeys wearing handcuffs on a trapeze. I am going to work you until the last second of your shift, lady!

I know the big guy is on his way, but I have another hour to get everything I want from you. I expect you to: sing me several songs, read through our entire collection of books (don't forget the voices or else you will need to start over), give me another bath because carrots don't come out quite as nicely as they go in, and waltz me around the house for as long as it entertains me. Don't expect any sympathy from me either.

Your day has been a cakewalk. Bathing and feeding all day. I mean really. You call that work? I do more work pulling those plants out of their pots. They are tricky ones. I plan to give you one last hoorah. When the bearded one arrives and you start telling him about your day, I will let it be known that your servitude was less than satisfactory!

The minute I hear the keys jingle at the door (aka the man's dinner bell), I will put on my best face. I don't know why you can't do the same. You could at least strain the peas out of your hair woman! When he walks in, I will crawl to him as fast as possible, as he is capable of fulfilling all my earthly desires. I like this one and his deep voice. His fuzzy face tickles my belly when he talks to me. Yours doesn't do that; you should fix that problem.

Go ahead and tell him all about how you had to please me the entire day. We both know I don't require much. You're the one, who like a lost puppy, fetches everything you find, half of which I never sent you to retrieve. I swear. I will coo at him like an adoring dove while you drone on about your 'daily demands.' He's not buyin' it.

The bearded one is amazing. He gets me laughing so hard by just talking to me. Move aside and stand witness to a real comic genius at work. Watch and learn. When he looks at me I am going to grin bigger than The Joker, showing him in one facial expression that I am absolute perfection in a pint-sized package. This is sure to instantly discredit your delusional discontent. Be prepared for me to toss a glare over at you, wrapping up our one-on-one time today with my smug look of satisfaction.

Dads are Parents, too

Man, it's an enormous job to be a mom. Thank God for the men, our male 'counterparents' (and all parenting partners for that matter)! After all, none of us could have babies without what men bring to the equation.

Stay with me, as I attempt to delve into the macho mystery that is the paternal psyche. I'm channeling my inner-man, beer in hand. Let's do this.

The big day has come for you and your little woman. Remember just don't call her big. You're remembering all the items on your 'Honey-Do' list as you simultaneously grab the stack of standby suitcases she's had waiting for weeks. That's when you realize *you* have nothing packed. You grope frantically for the first thing you see that is yours and stash it, and those celebratory cigars, into one of her bunch of bags. You mutter, *"This'll do,"* and help push your panting prego toward the door.

As you lower her into the car with the utmost care, it occurs to you that there will be one more with you on the ride home. You're practically pulling away when you hear something on the roof. It's the car seat! Gonna need that. You stop short of slamming on the brakes and ejecting your wife. Who signed me up for this anyway?

You make it to the hospital without an incidence of unexpected auto-delivery. Good, because since your interstate of mind is racing at 100 M.P.H. you probably couldn't handle the road and the woman all at once. Maybe you just lucked out and your kid came specially equipped with his own set of anti-lock brakes. But he can't stop from coming any longer.

Upon arriving at the hospital, you're introduced to the hardest quiz you've ever seen. *"My wife could give birth any moment and I can't even remember our zip code."* After filling out both of your life histories, your wife is finally getting situated in the labor room.

As every monitoring device known to Machine City is attached to her, the long process of waiting for your 'one' begins. There's no point trying to get any peace and quiet though, with all the beeping and buzzing your wife is now the penultimate baby noisemaker to your baby's first cry. In the midst of all the sound stew is your little being's heartbeat, rising and falling in anticipation along with your own. Hey, maybe we are related.

Now to commence with the hard part. *"Apple of my eye, my ass. The way she's screaming, it's got to be a watermelon."* Until now, you had no idea the mother of your child could speak in tongues, swear like an ironworker or make noises you thought were not humanly possible. Even though you have been rehearsing this script for weeks you are suddenly unsure whether you are prepared for this role.

The doctors come in. *"You're going to do what to my wife?"* You're wondering how many times that dog and pony show is going to happen before your baby finally arrives. You realize you just have to go with the flow, like the gush of amniotic fluid that just soaked you down to your socks and underwear.

Once those six doctors finish looking her over you exclaim, *"12 hours more? We've already been here a day!"* You hate to admit it, but you are now looking for a way out. Your heightened state comes to a halt as it occurs to you that you are not the only one who wants out. You've just bonded with your son--before he is even born!

Finally 'it' arrives. You witness the birth of a baby and it looks nothing like what you expected. It's more like a cross between Benjamin's Button, Ackroyd's cone like cranium, and *the* heinous Alien. You momentarily believe you have spawned a monster. As the legion of doctors and nurses lean in you witness his gripping survival instinct. The babe swats away furiously with the might of the Great Bambino. *"That's my boy."*

Finally, one of the nurses acknowledges your somewhat small, but vital role in this entire event by asking if you would like to cut the cord. You hesitantly agree, feeling it is your fatherly duty. You have a sudden revelation: this kid has had a rent-free existence until now; he's being ripped from his happy home, thus severing his only chance for true freedom for the rest of his life. As you clip your newborn's cord, you realize you have terminated all future calls to womb service, thereby setting him on his own path of responsibility. You whisper, *"Time to get a job, little buddy."*

Sitting in the hospital holding your freshly birthed child, you breathe in his underlying scent of placental juices. It's a fragrance unlike any that has dared to pass through your nostrils. Eau de' Calvin Slime, freshly bottled.

Had another dad described what you were about to go through before you actually did, you would have bet mad money that you would find yourself waking up on the floor. But, you defied the odds. And in doing so, you learned your first lesson from your newly arrived offspring--that you are even tougher than you thought!

Just one problem, you notice your wife in full-blown mommy mode, blissfully nursing your infant and it hits you. It's on between you and the boy!! Who's gonna win mommy's affection? It'll be hard, but I guess we'll just have call it a draw and split the prize.

You're beaming with pride at your most magnificent creation. You have decided to refer to yourself as Da Vinci or maybe Leonardo or perhaps just Da Leo for short. You don't see what the big deal is about this whole birthing thing.

You immediately get online to purchase every 'Fastest Swimmer,' 'Baby Making is my Thing,' and 'Miso Cute' shirt known to Man and woMAN kind so you can share your impeccable progeny with the world.

Doctor, Doctor, Read All About It

When human babies are born, just the sight of them melts your heart. Babies are sweet and vulnerable. Everything about them is designed to ensure they will be nurtured to survive. It's incredible that these mini-miracles grow into the creatures they do! Can I get a whoop, whoop?

Think about it--if we birthed hairy, fully-grown men, I don't believe we could guarantee them the same loving care. Do you?

There's this thing that happens when you go in for a hospital stay. Let's call it the Hospital Vacuum Tube Syndrome (HVTS) where the outside world somehow ceases to exist while you are there.

Here we were again, for the third time. I was already two kids in and had just met my yet to be named Grunt baby. We were happily enveloped in our HVTS, just overflowing with emotion, taking in our new baby. I couldn't have been happier. This new little being was finally in my arms and had instantly captivated my soul. I'd like to believe the feeling was mutual. You be the judge.

Our beautiful bubble was burst when one of the dozens of doctors we had already seen, was back once *again* to check on our newborn son. It's quite common when babies are born for them to be scrutinized to ensure they are 'up to code,' but this guy was showing a little too much interest. He waltzed in, grabbed my little bundle of boy and began undressing him. I watched him, impatiently, maternal instincts in overdrive, wanting my baby back. He uttered an "Uh oh" and I swear my heart stopped. I bolted upright in my open-backed handkerchief and immediately, but meekly asked, "What does uh oh mean?"

He began probing our son in an area that I was sure should not be poked as he muttered, "Hypospadias." I wondered what language he was speaking. My brain certainly wasn't functioning at full capacity after my body had just shot out a human cannon ball. "Hippo what-ee-us?" I said.

The doctor glared at me as though I were a moron. I reacted in my mind. "Hey, doc, do you see an MD after my name?" He began to describe how my son's urethra was incorrectly positioned. I nodded as though I had a clue what he was saying until he announced,

"His pee-hole is in the wrong spot."

"Oh no," was the only reaction I could muster I was so shocked. All I could think was, "How could I have given my son a pee-hole in the wrong place? How could I do this to this poor boy?" I had never even heard of anything like this before. Leave it to me to do something like this.

As blame and possible causes for this 'defect' were flying through my head, the doctor began to describe a plan of action. In a few months, we can take him to have surgery and correct his problem. The procedure may take a few hours, but he should be fine afterward.

No parent EVER wants to hear these words! This is the way it was and of course, it was all my fault. He diapered our baby and departed as quickly as he had arrived. We sat there absorbing what we had just seen and heard. Guilt was showering over me. I started cradling my sweet boy and apologizing to him as if I had somehow caused this unfortunate condition. The kid is going to hate me. I just knew it.

Our hospital vacuum-sealed tube had just had a blast of unwanted air pushed into it and I was not going to swallow it!

The second I got home, I was on the computer. What is this 'hippo-spade-e-us' and what can we do about it? I started frantically Googling every article on hippo-sape-pee-us that I could find. I was becoming an expert in pee-hole positioning.

Finally, my husband came in and shut the computer off. He told me there was nothing I could do about it and it would all work out. Being a mother, and a woman, my immediate reaction was, "Oh, what do you (and your correctly positioned pee-hole) know anyway?"

That same week I scheduled an appointment with our trusted pediatrician. I was hoping she would tell me our newest addition was just fine. I could feel the worry eating away inside me as I thought about the surgery and the pain it would no doubt inflict on my baby boy.

We took him to our doctor, and the moment she walked in my fears and tears came flooding out in my state of distress. As I spilled my concerns, she calmly examined him and announced, "He does not have a Hypospadias." Wait, what? Perhaps, I need to educate her on what exactly a Hypospadias is. I am an expert now--Kid Tested, Doctor Unapproved, after all.

I pointed out the small detail that lead the male doctor to the diagnosis of Hypospadias. He was a man after all, so he deserved the benefit of the doubt, right? Wrong.

She looked again and said, "I don't see it, but let's get my colleague in here for another opinion." Sounded good to me, because at this point, I felt like I was going to need at least five more of those '2nd' opinions.

Doctor number two came in and we finally got it, 'it' being a perfectly positioned all-natural pee-hole; one that has optimal peeing capability. Thank goodness, because I really wasn't sure how many more times I could explain that one again.

Mom Prob: What to do when hit with potentially bad news about your baby?

a. Question authority!!! Remember, you (and your insurance company) pay the salaries of the medical professionals tending to your child's health. They work for you. No matter how uninformed, young and/or inexperienced you are, you have the right and the power to research to decide what is best for your child.
b. As a parent, you are more in tune with your child than you may realize. Listen to your instincts. Ask questions. Most importantly if you feel something is not right don't let anyone else tell you it is.
c. Doctors are humans. They make mistakes, too. It is your right and your responsibility to take an active and informed role in the decision making process. Always seek a second opinion, at the very least!
d. Remember Google is your friend. Google knows stuff we're not smart enough to ask. Just remember not everything Google knows is the total truth. Don't allow yourself to be drawn into the endless abyss that is the Internet. Seek trusted sites with knowledgeable, validated sources. If you are not discerning on the Internet, your fears WILL run away with you!
e. Even if, as in my case, you know very little about a problem, you will learn at lightning speed in situations such as these. It's just one of the many ways kids teach us and help make us better people.

It was an auspicious beginning to life with Alexander the Grunt and there has been nary a dull moment since. Speaking of dull Grunt moments, let's see what else he has to say during his day.

Day is done but not for Grunt

I know what you're thinking as nighttime comes...your day is finally over. Well, think again lady. I'll be sure to wake you up several times throughout the night and grimace at you as you half-asleep/half-awake run into my crib. I know you won't turn the light on in the hopes that I will fall right back to sleep. The images of your late night mishaps always sweeten my dreams.

I plan to be as quiet as possible while you grope the walls of the darkest room in existence. I like the lingering sound of your stifled cries when you stub your toes on all the corners you never saw coming. I don't really need anything, but I do want to keep you on your (now throbbing) toes.

You never know when that monster under the bed is going to pop out. I take comfort in knowing that if he sees your unkempt, frazzled hair, bloodshot eyes, and grotesquely swollen feet, you will surely send him scampering back into hibernation.

Thanks for scaring the monsters away, Mom. I would hate to have to do that for myself. Being a busy baby, I have enough on my plate as it is.

Mmmm. Plate. How about a midnight snack while you're up?

Good night, odd lady. I can't wait to begin our challenging game all over again tomorrow.

Little House on the Parkway

Let's Get Ready to Tumble

In our house, three children means there is three times the trouble. Hard to imagine, I know. The kids can fight over a broken doll that has lain in the toy box since the dawn of toys. Their battle is one of territory and dominance. As they struggle, one rolling around like a crocodile with prey in its jaws, screams shatter against the walls like a slain action figure once did during a previous battle. Elbows are flying and feet are flailing. Eventually someone takes a hit to the eye. A novice parent might jump at this sight, but having three children I am no novice. That's my story and I'm sticking to it.

I have learned that with every elbow to the eye there is an equal and opposite pulling of the hair to be had. An ordinary parent simply cannot keep up with the bodily damage that is done on a daily basis. There are those rare occasions where the loser wails at the winner (aka the elbower) and the winner concedes with a truce. Sometimes parental intervention is all that will cause them to pause. Most of the time, the Super Dome immediately launches into another of its infamous sports.

If I sit down, the kids will trample over one another to clamor onto Mt. Mommy. Then they begin the precision attack of wedging the others out. Feet and legs stretch slowly into rib cages and eventually even Mt. Mommy shifts under the pressure.

I am their 'Braveheart' and they must fight until a winner is named. The hardest part about this battling is there is no period of mourning for those who have been lost in combat. No trumpets sound, alerting that the next round of fighting is about to erupt either. At this point, I would even take the forewarning of a kilt-clad horseman.

Even the smallest person in our house lets it be known that he can't be pushed around. That is why he grunts….all the time!

There is Alexander the Grunt the Amasser of Unconquered Lands, the Builder of Bridges, and the Destroyer of Dinners. There's also Ding-Ding the Lord of Laughter, and Creator of Chaos. I can't forget Kiki the Lady of the Cake, she who speaks in whispers and riddles.

If I'm ever bored (which never happens as you can see) I just sit back and watch a little live action war-play. My daughter shouts out commands to a non-existent fleet, "Ready for the attack." Ding-Ding, in all his glory, steadies his light-saber and prepares for the coming hordes. As the imaginary swordsmen heed their orders, the Grunt steps in like a well-oiled Sumo Wrestler.

Ding-Ding, being cornered on both sides, goes for the obvious move and attempts to restrain the Grunt with nothing but his bare hands. He has made a poor decision. The Grunt cannot be boy-handled. He can hardly be manhandled for that matter, just ask his dad.

The Grunt has enlisted his most trustworthy defensive measure, the squirmy worm. He is a limp noodle flapping in the tiny arms of his some-what bigger brother.

Ding-Ding begins to totter at the weight of this toddler and he now realizes the horrible mistake he's made. His eyes look to me as though I am able to save him from this frivolous fight with a slight wave of my hand. I look on in eager anticipation, while eating my popcorn, to see how this battle will conclude.

Somehow, the Grunt has found freedom, but Ding-Ding is not yet ready to give up his cause. He jumps into the pit and they begin pacing one another. They look to each other and pause to appreciate the cheers of the surrounding crowd. Kiki sees that she has been overlooked for far too long and she too joins in this clumsy dance of war.

Once in the heat of a most epic battle, it is as though they are speaking some hidden language. There is silence as they size one another up. As their eyes are locked onto one another, tension permeates this pit of doom. Eyes are darting furiously back and forth and heads begin shaking between them. Some critical decision is being made no doubt on a tactical plan of action.

Suddenly, the two oldest turn to me and say in unison, "We want some popcorn, please." Grunt, grunts along in agreement.

It's survival of the fittest at its finest.

The Fridge Phantom

Sometimes I forget things. This is by far my most annoying fault. I used to have the photographic memory of an elephant. I called her Peanut. Ah the good old' days. Okay, perhaps that is a bit of an exaggeration, but my memory was amazing. As recently as nine years ago, I could remember all of my high school friends' phone numbers (yes, back when you actually had to dial phone numbers). My first child was born nine years ago. Coincidence? I think not.

All of my useless information was once stored like gold bullion in Fort Knox. Children have the knack for diminishing your memory in such a way that you aren't clear whether it's really them or if a Man in Black got to you first. Where are your slick sunglasses when you need them?

This is what happens when your memory and parenthood collide!

Our fridge has two settings, door opening avalanche or cavernous black hole. We can debate the legitimacy of that statement later. I said, 'later,' not when. The point is the thing goes from one extreme to the other.

I am a food hoarder. I hate to have food go bad and yet I hate the idea of an empty fridge. I always want to have a variety of snacks and treats for the kids. It may be a mom thing, or maybe it's just a crazy me thing. You decide.

I went to the store and stocked our fridge to its breaking point. Food was on top of food, making food babies. Dirty food! I'll stop there to keep this PG. I felt great about having a full fridge. That was one less thing for me to worry about. Believe me I need to lessen my worry load as often as I can.

Mom Prob: Don't worry, be happy is a lot easier said than done.

We can (often) make things more difficult than they need to be.
a. Take time for you and your family to just relax and enjoy unscheduled family moments together.
b. Don't overschedule activities or impose unnecessary responsibilities on your family and your life.
c. Decide to live fully, but not fearfully. Don't be afraid you are not making everyone else happy. Needless worry will only wear you down.

A few days passed and I began noticing several foods perishing before their expiration date. I was perturbed. I inspected every item in the fridge and cleaned it out. Then I cursed the store with all of my breath. The term 'when in doubt, blame Wal-Mart' can be very soothing to an irritated Mom. Still, my love/hate relationship with the grocery magnate endures.

The next day I noticed more food had gone bad. I knew something was definitely wrong. I felt a wave of panic as major appliance expenses began going off in my head like an alarm. I began an investigation. We like those 'round these parts.

Everything looked fine. The seals were intact; the door had been completely shut. I know I couldn't have possibly bought an entire trip's worth of spoiled items. Hmmm. Think, Mommy, think.

I looked at the little knob, you know the knob, or maybe yours is a dial. In real terms, it's the thermostat that regulates the temperature aka, the 'controller of cold.' Well, it had been turned way down. That meant the temperature in the fridge went up. Up is down? I feel a deep connection with this appliance at this moment.

I realize it must have been me all along. I recall the cheese I just threw out and suddenly little bloated bellies begin dancing around my head, like pitchfork wielding Tweety birds. I curse myself as I consider all the starving…oh you get the sad picture. Yes, I made a mental apology to the store, as I turned the knob back up. Fridge be damned.

Grocery day comes again. I restock the fridge and start to do my relaxed breathing. Breathe…1…2…3. A day or two pass and everything is frozen! It's like in that animated movie all the kids are talking about, except there aren't any singing snowmen providing me comic relief. Everything, I am talking fridge, freezer, and even the door handle were covered in frosty crystals.

You know, the white crystalline icicles that somehow burn the food even though you don't necessarily understand the logic of it all. The lovely, 'you really shouldn't eat me now, but I know you will stand here for a minute or 10 before you make your final decision' kind of icicles. At this point, I just know it couldn't have been me. Not again. I learned my lesson the first time. Didn't I?

I came to the only possible conclusion in a household of three children and two adults: there is a ghost in the fridge! And, it doesn't want us to eat.

Determined not to let this demon spirit destroy my dinners, I start googling ghost finding equipment. As I am looking into EVP recorders at 5 am, I hear something.

Why am I on the internet at 5 am, you ask? It couldn't possibly be because there was an apparition in the house and I was up all night on ghost guard under my blanket shield, could it? That isn't at all what happened though because I er... What I really meant is, we moms have to grab those uninterrupted moments to surf the web when we can get them, which isn't when the kids are up, that's for sure. Yeah, that is exactly what I meant.

Back to the noise coming from the kitchen, I put down the laptop and slid out of bed as quietly as I could. This ghost was about to be caught. I started to wonder if I should have invested in a net like they do in the cartoons. What do spirits feel like? Are they slippery, slimy, or sticky? Perhaps they are a combination of all of that. I may just find out. I wondered if I should touch it or even if I could?

I peeked out the door. Nothing. I crept down the hallway silently cursing the creaking house, which was obviously in cahoots with this poltergeist as it was betraying my every step. Yes, we have officially moved up the specter spectrum from ghost to poltergeist.

The strange noises persist, so the poltergeist is unaware of my impending ambush. Tiptoeing in my bathrobe, I am determined to catch Casper in the act and clobber him back into the afterlife. I make it to the kitchen and there, standing before me is the fridge-door wide open. Aha. If only I had that net or a camera to catch this ghost in in the act!

As I close the door, I hear more suspicious noises coming from the living room. Carefully I sneak in to investigate. I'm getting good at this phantom detecting stuff. Guess it comes with the territory, but I don't remember seeing it on the job description.

Come to think of it, I don't recall a job description at all. If I had, I wonder if I would have more carefully considered taking this motherhood job in the first place? Would you?

As I round the corner, I see half a stick of butter on the floor. Not the butter! This ghost has gone too far now. Paula Deen would be livid.

I jump out from around the corner and yell, "I caught you!" at the top of my lungs. My Ding-Ding child looks up at me in surprise. There he was, leaned back against our black armchair, cowboy style, with nothing on but his underwear. He was propped up on his elbows looking as laid back and innocent as any kid possibly could.

In one hand, he is holding the remote trying to get the TV to turn on. In his other hand is the missing half of the abandoned stick of butter left conspicuously on the floor. He sits licking it like a lollipop, looking at me as if I am the one who is nuts. For a split second, I see a resemblance to my son. Holding it in the air he announces, "My lubber."

He admitted to the fridge tampering easily enough. Sadly, there will be no more ghost-hunting in my immediate future. The best thing is that I found the fridge fiend before disaster struck and any real harm was done, like food poisoning or me suing Wal-Mart for selling bad food.

As a temporary fix, we enlisted the use of all-purpose duct tape to keep the refrigerator door closed. It was a cheap and handy alternative to those darned childproof locks. Yes, they make those too. Apparently kids will get into anything. Maybe I'll get one someday. If only I could figure out how to get the thing open now!

MOMent: I bought all of these safety locks to keep my children out of danger and what happened was I locked myself out.

After the struggle to figure out how to use these things, my youngest just used his brute force and baby weight to literally rip them in two. I've put cleaners so high up that I felt like I was up in the attic when I was getting them. I've gone chic-baby minimalist and had nothing but a sofa and floor in our living room. The truth is, unless kids are in a padded cell, there is always a way to get hurt because they can even get hurt on themselves. Sigh. It's a miracle we humans have survived to overpopulate the planet. Be aware and be cautious. Know your safety boundaries, know where your children are at all times, and most importantly know what they are capable of doing. (Which is get into any and everything!) Teach them to listen and then speak to them about what they can do and what they should not do. It is hard work. It is an everyday repetition, and you must be vigilant because their safety and your peace of mind (and house) is at stake.

When Bras Attack...

All kids find ways to create problems that parents would never have imagined were possible. We eventually learn that everything can be dangerous when used by children. Socks are choking hazards when shoved into your brother's mouth. Ceiling fans are spinning wheels of destruction when you forcefully throw objects into them. Cribs can be akin to Chinese Finger Traps for chunky little legs.

Anything can be dangerous due to a child's inexperience in using it. We are constantly being reminded how unsuspecting everyday items can easily transform into torture devices.

Before my shower the other night, I hung some clothes on my doorknob. Have I mentioned showers are a luxury? Well, I left a bra hanging on the door handle and the Grunt managed to crawl through one of the straps. I heard his 'grying', you know, angry grunting and crying.

I immediately grabbed my iPhone to take pictures of the 'bra on boy' match. I was actually impressed with my quick thinking; normally I just save the kids and miss the photo ops. This area needs improvement because people are highly skeptical of my Family Tales when I don't have the photographic evidence to back up the stories.

While he was fighting the bra, I couldn't help but laugh at the irony of the age-old battle between men and the enigmatic item that is the 'bra.' In a fleeting moment, I have a vision of his future, his innocence peeling away, him dating, him intentionally wrestling with a bra and then I choke up. Who knew a perplexing piece of attire could stir such a reaction?

The whole scene was actually quite traumatizing for the both of us, really. Once rescued, I offer the stern motherly advice that he should never be anywhere near a bra ever again.

The moral of the story is that humor can balance out even the most serious situations. Had Grunt had more balance, that bra would not have attacked him in the first place. Boys...

30 Days of Might

I must admit, there are certain aspects of parenting that I did not believe in before I actually became one. We all have this sense of who we will be as a parent before we get to that point.

I recall the many things I swore I would never do. But I distinctly remember realizing how uninformed my pre-parent brain actually was. I laughed at that naive girl who thought she knew something about having children. I laughed at her ignorance. I laughed and laughed and laughed and…. Sorry. I laughed for just a bit longer than I probably should have.

We had two children. One, two, yes, we had two children. Oops had to get out the fingers to double check the math on that one. Then we decided, without ever actually discussing it, to have another baby. He entered our two-child home like a wound-up warthog and shook our world, and our schedules, in a way we never anticipated.

Our grunt baby was sent to knock a whole new level of sense into us. He proved to us that we could venture far beyond what we ever imagined into the realm of, "What was I thinking?"

We now had two boys in diapers, no sleep, no energy, no me-time, no idea what the outer world was like anymore, and we were surrounded by lovable little people who reminded us of 'someone that I used to know.'

I was in love, fully immersed in love, but at the same time, I could feel my brain cells dividing and wafting away into oblivion. Bye-bye brain cells.

One of the major contributors to that process is breast-feeding. Few people understand how much a woman sacrifices to provide the best she can for her baby. Nursing is more than a chore, it is a commitment. It is a tedious and time-consuming investment well worth making. I commend all mothers who choose to do it.

I decided once again to breastfeed with my third baby. He had a hard time latching on, so eventually I resorted to using a pump. The baby's feedings are every 2-3 hours for about the first month in order to establish a good milk supply. The more he drinks, the more you make.

Let me repeat the important part of that sentence, *every 2-3 hours*. That means you pump when you wake up, and two hours after that you must pump again, two hours after that, and so on all through the day and night for one month.

Mom Prob: One month is 30 days.

Did you know 30 days has a total of 720 hours in it. A typical breastfeeding session takes about 15-25 minutes and can vary slightly. So of that 720 hours you need to take out say, 20 minutes every two hours. What you are left with is...a shell of an existence. I was deprived on more than a few levels, the main two being sleep and energy deprivation. That is a very bad deprivation combination. Say that 10 times fast. It's difficult, especially when sleep deprived.

To Zzzzz or Not to Zzzzzz

The Grunt Baby has been the most difficult of all of our children so far. He's young yet. There may be hope. He is as headstrong as he is precious and as willful as he is stubborn. He is particularly obstinate about sleeping. Quite simply, he refuses.

Both of our first two babies started sleeping through the night at about one month. I guess you can only get lucky so many times. The Grunt was not going to go quietly into this mold. He was determined to let us know that he was going to be his very own unique person.

The husband and I were accustomed to our sweet babies who slumbered peacefully all night long. We were spoiled and our bubble was about to be busted by this bull-headed baby boy.

I should have known the first night in the hospital that he was just not interested in this waste of time known as sleeping. I tried everything. I put him on my chest so he could hear my heartbeat. I laid him beside me, curled up next to my stomach, to keep him warm. I tried the bassinet. I caressed him next to my face. I sang my own versions of lullabies. I cooed at him. I rocked him. I cried with him (probably the most of all those things).

Nothing was making him happy. Nothing, except for his daddy, that is. Daddy finally rescued the little prisoner that was trapped within me for nine months. The moment daddy laid down with him our baby was at ease. He slept on daddy's chest as if he had finally made it home after an arduous journey (of about nine months). I knew then that this was daddy's boy. I also knew that this did not bode well for me. That was the first night I met...with the Wrath of Grunt.

Sleeping has always been one of my favorite pastimes. If it was a professional sport, I could be the Lebron James or the Kobe Bryant. No? Well, I could be awesome at it and make lots of money.

The point is I love my sleep. I tend to have a hard time falling asleep even when I'm exhausted, but I LOVE it and Grunt HATES it. So you see, there is an inborn conflict here. Not sure this is going to end well.

Mom Prob: You can be too tired to fall asleep.

Your brain can be in non-stop mode while your body begs for a reboot. Try some chamomile, Valerian tea, or exercise until you literally pass out. All of the above.

The actual act of sleeping makes me quite happy. Grunt was determined from birth, to make me appreciate every nanosecond of sleep for the rest of my life. Here's what our nightly schedule was to show you what I mean.

The Grunt would go to sleep from 8:00- 11:30pm. I stayed up every night until then to feed him. This was the latest I could manage and still be functional enough to finish what I hadn't been able to do during the day. If I was lucky, I might be able to fall exhaustedly into bed by midnight.

Falling asleep was a different story... I would feed him, stick him back in the bed, finish my stuff, and exhaustedly fall into bed.

At about 3:00am I would wake to feed him again. I had to do it just right, otherwise the Grunt would take silent night feedings as playtime. No lights and being as swift as possible were critical to the success of this operation.

I'm about as coordinated and graceful as two conjoined cats attacking in different directions. And, I do NOT possess any Ninja skills--don't let my looks fool you. Believe me, there was many a late night with swearing fests due to these shortcomings.

At around 5:30am he would wake again grunting for another bottle. I would take his earlier bottle (only ¼ of which he drank) and throw it out. To appease my conscious I'd shake my head for a second at the thought of those 30 minutes of sleep I lost for no reason not to mention the breast milk and the additional time I spent pumping.

Then I'd turn his lamp on so that he could play for a bit in his crib while I desperately tried to piece together a few patches of rest. All of this led to me hoping to get some semblance of a whole nights rest. Piecing sleep together is exactly as it 'seams'--like sewing a quilt with no fabric. If that quilt does somehow work in some way, it sure as h-e double hockey sticks won't keep you warm!

All Through the Town

On the Road Uh, When?

There is a natural ebb and flow of energy when you are a parent. Usually that flow is in one direction-out! The oddest aspect of the ever-puzzling energy dilemma is the fact that no matter how much sleep you manage to get, you will probably never wake up feeling well rested. This is partially because as a parent nothing ever goes quite as planned. Perhaps some part of you hoards a large reserve of energy to help you stay ever vigilant in the fight against the unexpected.

I can vaguely recall mornings that were lazily filled with nothing more than lax habits. I remember the days long ago, when I could walk around my spotless house or even just take my sweet time getting dressed.

Ah, getting dressed. That is among my fondest memories. I think of my clothes that were once hung neatly in my closet. They were organized by color, ROYGBIV style, because there was more than enough time to make sure that slightly darker shade of violet sat behind its fuchsia counterpart

I once savored my hot tea as I perused my perfectly pressed apparel, until I found the ideal ensemble. I always left the house with an air of cool confidence concerning my hair and makeup. But the best part was returning home to a neat house with everything in its place! Ah, those were the days-- organized, quiet and never rushed.

Those days are gone.

They became nothing more than distant memories once children invaded my tidy little world.

One child is an adjustment. Your morning schedule extends at least an extra 30 minutes so you can get ready for the day. Making sure your sweet baby has been properly prepared for the outing is a feat unto itself. You have a full bag of extra this-and-thats, just in case. Time is on your side as you double-check yourself to be sure that you aren't forgetting anything. You are a Mom, or Dad, on a roll. Get the butter.

You step out your door with both you and baby looking cute as ever in your brand new matching outfits. Ah, Success. Envious eyes everywhere look you over because, let's face it, you've got it goin' on, girl! Even you are impressed.

Let's take it up a notch, to two children. No big deal, right?

You have just upped your ante in a big way.

After the first child, each additional child will require one hour of personalized prep time. You also have to factor in that extra 'just in case' quotient, because a boy just wouldn't be a boy without it.

Here's what I mean. Both kids are dressed. You're just finishing her hair, your son walks in squishing auburn goo in his little fist. In his other hand, he holds your lipstick without the tube! He's turned your favorite 'Sinful Sienna' into a self-tanner, covering all exposed areas of skin with it. You marvel at how evenly he's applied his unintentional 'fake' tan.

Back to the skin-tastrophy at hand. Miraculously, you manage to remove most of it except for two lingering spots on either cheek. Throughout your day, at least 10 people comment that, "His skin just glows!" The miracle of makeup!

You muffle a snicker as it tries to sneak past your lips. As you utter 'thank you' you contemplate whether your sons 'mishap-plication' should become the new standard for all your skincare needs. Apparently, no one would be the wiser.

I also noticed that two children somehow cause mom to triple check everything. Walking out the door, you can't help but feel like you are forgetting something. You have now resorted to the post-it notes wallpaper to make sure your mommy brain can handle all of the added extras.

Getting *to* the car is a major feat. Getting *into* the car with everything and everybody is even harder. It's right up there with loading a clown car--only they're all related to you and have carry-on luggage twice their size. When you are out, people look at you in awe as that accomplished, got-it-all-together mother with an ideal family and wonder how you do it. If only they knew, right?

Add another kid into the mix and what you get is *chaos*. Pure and simple CHAOS. Let's just be frank here.

Waking up, you find yourself lying in bed hoping that you'll get a last minute cancellation in your jam-packed schedule for the day. The alternative is a battle that seems to be stuck on repeat. Not only is it on repeat but the TV is busted and you can't get the (insert expletive) thing to turn off anymore!

Having three kids goes a little like this. If you have yet to experience it, put yourself in my shoes for this scenario. You lay in bed an extra 10 minutes silently cursing yourself the entire time, knowing you are only worsening the impending doom that will soon be your mo(u)rning. Still you lay there, silently scolding yourself and then you begin to sing all of the words to *The Jefferson's* theme song. Do you know why? Does anyone know why at this point?

Philosophical prattle bumps around in your head for an extra two minutes before you jerk yourself back to the real world. Finally, you flop out of bed, falling straight to the floor because you need the sudden jolt of something that coffee just doesn't pack anymore. You jump up and make it into the first sector of the battlefield. Checkpoint reached.

Mom Prob: As a parent, every morning involves the decision of whether or not you should put 'real people' clothes on.

I always gauged my outfit by my kids' ages and the day's activity. Infants destroy designer wear. The only job interview you should show up to in your pajamas should be a mattress testing position. Let me know if you don't get the job, or if they have any more positions available.

Now it is time to start the feeding frenzy. Even though you have the bacon and eggs ready and plated, the first two begin to rant at you since they consider pancakes the 'breakfast of champions.' You find yourself having a familiar argument over the existence of said pancakes and realize that kid logic is so much better than grown-up logic due to the absence of sense. Who needs things to make sense anyway?

Part of you drifts back to lying in bed, oh, so long ago. At this point, it occurs to you that force-feeding may become option number 1. As you imagine the scene, you consider what it might look like to a stranger.

A slightly harder than slight shake of the head brings you back to reality. Option number 1 may not be the most motherly of choices.

The oldest is somewhat capable of getting dressed. She still has the occasional stray shoe on the wrong foot but she can at least pull the clothing on and look like she wasn't dressed in a dark room while blindfolded and bound.

Once you see her choice of outfit, you furiously nod in approval and send her into the next target zone. She is dressed, so you use child labor to have her search the boy's room for whatever clothes he hasn't devoured yet. Being the little monster that he is, that must be what is happening because they just keep disappearing!

As she digs through the rubble of his room, you get to work on the youngest. You silently send up a prayer that she can handle him without you, as you face the fresh load that has just been dumped on you—the one in baby's diaper.

Great. Now he'll need *another* bath. A verbal cue would have sufficed, but this one is a man of action. As a parent, you know you should appreciate that. But, in this moment you just can't. You cry a little on the inside, because you just know that was most likely his last clean outfit.

Now, what to do with the other two who are ready? If they come into the bathroom where I can keep an eye on them, they are sure to be drenched in no time. The thought of having to begin the whole process over again with all three is almost too much to bear.

You pause for a moment and ask yourself if it is really all that important to take this excursion after all. Oh, that's right, the oldest going to school, the middle child going to the preschool (for which you paid a handsome ransom) and the little one will have a meltdown if he misses his play date... There is no turning back.

The three are all dressed and fed and now you begin gathering the day's supplies. Your purse has become a med kit, toy box, restaurant, art studio, laundry mat, and camping supply store. Yet, with all that, you still have this suspicion you are undersupplied.

Time to load the car down with a month's worth of who-knows what for each child, because the moment you decide to leave an item behind is exactly when you will need it. When you have three kids, more is *always* the only option. Remember that.

As you finally make your way out the door with that defeated blank stare on your once optimistic face, you no longer worry about what you are forgetting. You have simply come to accept the fact that you have forgotten at least half of the items you need to survive the day. But hey, give yourself a pat on the back. Just finding your way out the door through sleep-deprived eyes is a triumph.

Mom Prob: It's been said that when you're pregnant, the chemistry of your brain changes in preparation for the care and feeding of your baby.

Despite the supposed shift, when baby arrives you still can't remember where you left the diaper wipes.

Hi, My name is Susie and I am a reminder-aholic. I scribble post-it notes and stick them all over the kitchen, bath, and nightstand, even in the car, but always out of reach of the little humans. If they got a hold of them, I would surely lose my mind.

Leave reminders and set timers on all your devices. But most importantly, keep your mind engaged. While an idle mind is said to be the devil's playground, a stagnate brain is the best friend of memory loss. Be warned!

The door shutting behind you is the sound of admission. You are no longer the organized, well-dressed, put together, accomplished mom that others secretly envy through their smiles. You are now the scavenger mom, half-frazzled and worn down, surrounded by a tiny army, sent by an unknown foe to tear you down, one long day at a time.

You are the mother that others part for like the Red Sea, partly out of pure pity since you were obviously tricked into having three kids, but mostly because of your crazed look of Mommydom. Honestly, you couldn't care less. You made it *and* you made them. The days of organization and color-coding can become tedious over time. Look what 'the days of your life' hold now...

They are now a wasteland of unexpecteds, half-dones, overlookeds, and forgottens. Your life is filled with smudges, smears, dirt, falls, laughter and hugs that make everything else fade into the background. You now have post it note color-coded walls instead of clothing. Your heart is filled from top to bottom, from morning to morning every day, with no lapses in between. Kisses are your currency of choice. You may be a mostly catatonic mother, but you my dear, are the mother to three angels that live and breathe your very soul.

Always remember --You are their everything and they are everything to you.

That's One Smooth Mommy

I took all three kids to the farmer's market the other day. Our farmer's market is wonderful. The kids love going and meeting people who actually grew the food from seed. Nice idea, but to attempt such a feat solo is risky--as in flight risk.

There are so many variables to take into account with an outing such as this, so I make an effort to simplify. I choose to use a single umbrella stroller; you know the kind that was the staple for mothers around 20 to 30 years ago? That was before the evolution of the luxury- complex-gadget-gimmick-ridden Cadillac versions of what we consider infant transportation today.

I opt for the single-mode stroller, not only because I am somewhat of a purest in my own mind, but also because the middleman does not want to be treated like a baby and would have nothing to do with a tandem stroller. This, of course, means that on outings he will settle for nothing less than being 'free range,' and that leaves a lot to chance.

Can this 3-year old savage be controlled away from the wild of his life at home? My daughter knows the rules and to stay close at hand, but this wild child goes beyond testing my limits.

The challenge begins, in my head, the moment we arrive as I anticipate my next steps. 'Who do I unload first? If I unload the man-child first, then I risk the chance of him actually running. If I unload the girl first, she could help unload the man-child, but even then, he is still a flight-risk. If I let her out first, is she old enough to guard the door and keep wild child from escaping until I get little one safely strapped into the stroller?'

High anxiety is setting in and we are not even out of the car yet. The kids are wondering why we've been sitting here for so long. Perhaps I should do something.

I go for the stroller; I load Sir Grunts-a-lot, and head around to the other side of the car. I lock the stroller in place and sit it beside my feet, turn to the still buckled boy and unload him from the car and put a vice grip hold on his hand. As I am unloading the known defector, the Grunt and my daughter are by my side. Phew. Did you get all of that? Just take it one kid at a time.

Ding-ding is questioning my every move and making sure that I am fully aware of his discontent. We then walk back around to the driver's seat, I grab my purse, double-check that I have my keys (you don't want to be locked out of your car with three kids, believe me) and lock the doors. We head in the direction of the market. Whew! Step 1 was taxing, but still a success.

Now I can breathe easy for a few seconds as we stroll to the market. The kids like the walking part, and they do a good job of staying with me...as long as they know my attention is focused on them. I still have to remind them every few seconds that my attention *is* still on them. It's a concentric circle.

First, I let the kids pick out an item they like. Today, they have chosen some homemade pies. Princess picks peach and the buster busts out that he wants blueberry. Grunt doesn't get any because he would just throw it at me since, at the time; he was still on a liquid diet. As they float in their temporary 'heaven,' gooey grins and all, I continue my pursuit of purchases by planning my next stops.

I gather my bags and by force of habit place them on the handles of the umbrella stroller along with my purse that feels like I have a few bricks from the new patio we are installing. Boy, am I glad I have this stroller to carry that load for me!

MOMent: When you are so ingenious as to create a use for an everyday object beyond its intended use.

I have a kid on either side and I am pushing the Grunt. Shoppers stop and do the usual 'goo-goo, ga-ga' to the baby, like he can understand their brand of silly non-mommy speak. The kids stop and pet every animal they see (or think they see) and not always in the same place at the same time. I am doing a great job keeping an eye on the two walkers at once.

I see the lady who sells culinary herbs and start shepherding them toward her. I had been wanting some Thyme so I push my way up to the counter and make a quick quip about how we all need a little more *Thyme* in our day. I mean, I had to. Just as I do, baby Grunt launches into a full on fit. Guess he didn't think it was funny. Screaming at the top of his lungs because we have stopped moving, I have no choice now but to pick him up or he will not stop.

A total recall of the countless times the contents on the back of an empty stroller have spilled when not being counterbalanced by a baby, is a highly developed Mommy skill. I have to quickly shift the weight of the objects into the seat, while at the same time seamlessly lifting the crying infant out. If not, in addition to suffering the humiliation of everyone looking to see what I am doing to my baby to make him cry soooooo hard, they would also be nosing around in my personal effects as they watch the kids tussle over and inquire about my lady items. Never again.

If you were watching this, you would surely weep. First, I point to both kids and then to my feet, marking the designated spots for them to remain during this maneuver. I methodically grab the bags off of the stroller in one hand; unbuckle Grunt with the other hand, while also scooping him up with that same hand. With my foot holding the stroller down on his footrest, and with him snug against me, I swing the bags into his seat. In a matter of seconds, I have successfully completed this entire feat. With the exception of one thing.

Two women are watching and one comments, "Wow, you really have all of that under control!" I figuratively pat myself on the back, and thank her with a smile. Strangers always like to comment on your parenting skills, or lack thereof.

Once I have soaked up the adulation, I quickly assess the current situation. Pocketbook in the stroller. Check. Grunt in my arms. Check. Kiki on her mark. Check. Ding-Ding on his mark beside her. Bags are secured. Check. Wait a second. Go back. Ding-Ding is gone!

My heart thuds against my chest wall. Panic bubbles up. I can feel it flushing my face as I look frantically in every direction for my little menace. My mind is racing with fears as I scour the scene for his tiny figure. About a football field away, I see a familiar impish head bobbing (Really, it was more like 20 feet, but my adrenaline has caused my imagination to go wild)!

I pull Grunt in closer, grab Kiki by the wrist, and start rushing through the crowd like a linebacker toward my little runaway. People are flung aside as I push through with urgency, munchkins in tow. I make it to Ding-Ding just as he is reaching for an open carton of eggs (of course), free-range (of course). He was probably going to liberate them. Either that or eat them.

The vendor leers at me. Not now, buddy. I have mothering to do. I instinctively squat down to look him in the eyes. As we are reunited, a wave of emotion begins to subside, but not before I squeeze the boy in a hug that feels tighter than any we've had before. He looks at me bewildered for a moment before pointing to the dozen new friends he just made. I gladly buy his eggs, collect my parcels and move on.

I'm not sure what you are thinking. Maybe you're not impressed with my handling of the situation. Let me tell you a secret though. A few seconds is the equivalent of an hour in a child's mind. No matter how prepared or aware of their capabilities you are, in less than a minute you can find yourself questioning everything you thought you had come to understand. I knew from the moment we decided to venture out that my wild child's main goal was to break the imaginary barricade I would impose on him. They wait for your weakest moment and then they strike. Sneaky little critters.

Back to the scene of the getaway. The egg vendor is not the only one who is giving me dirty looks. Considering the extenuating circumstances, I may have to resort to my standby situation diffuser. That's where you feign that you don't speak English. We use what skills we have... I have very few.

Speaking of Stores & Stories

Let's face it; a large part of parenting consists of either reading or telling stories. With three children, I have done so much of it that, at times, it becomes my reality.

For example, recounting this routine trip to the store turned into a tale reminiscent of Dr. Seuss:

Once upon a time,
There was a dainty 2-year-old girl,
Her eyes of deep green, could stop the world.
This little girl as precious, as any could be,
Her cheeks still chubby, just like a new baby.
Her face was as innocent, an angel not of sin,
That is where our story does begin.

Her mother had been teaching her numbers.
When it began, it was quite encumbered.
The two would count from 1 to 10,
Start at the beginning and repeat it again,
They'd say those numbers in hefty amounts.
The sequence said too many times to count.

Insistent they were, 'til success was achieved,
'Twas prize time for her, and Mommy relief.
"To Target We Go," off to find a new toy,
To mark the success of their teaching ploy.
Once they got to the big red store,
A search ensued for a cart to score.

The little girl pointed for her Mommy to look,
Her tiny finger bent in the shape of a crook
She motioned to the huge 'kid' shopping cart.
Mommy's eyes gazed at the aisles of the mart,
Back at the cart for the smallest of persons.
She knew this quick trip had just worsened.

The little girl was seated all snug as a bug,
Her Mommy had this wheeled boulder to lug.
The duo began to browse all the toys,
While little Bo Peep did not make a noise.
Mommy cautiously rounded the corners,
The girl sought something special to join her.

Their oversized wagon crept down the aisles,
It seemed they'd travelled a 100-plus miles.
Finally, the sweet child made her decision.
She picked the toy she long had envisioned,
A purple clad doll gripped in her hand.
Mommy hastened her trusty exit plan.

As the three headed to checkout of this place,
They noticed many people filled this space.
They got in line to pay and wait their turn,
The doors so near; for freedom they yearned.
They waited patiently after their search,
Counting the time 'til they'd own this merch.

"One, two, customers buying anew,
Three, four, they all walked out the door.
We're after five, we've almost arrived,"

The store was quiet, no one made a sound,
The girl yelled "Six-Six-Six" turning 'round,
She shrieked at the top of her lungs.
All stopped, the sounds flew from her tongue.
Embarrassed Mommy turned white as a bear,
The girl's squealing caused others to stare,

They slunk ahead on the sounds possession.
Her girl repeated the numbers in procession.
Mom squirmed as all eyes looked on,
Shock, disapproval, judgement and beyond,
They paid and bounded through the door.
As they did so, Mommy softly swore-

"They'd never return, no, never more."

What's for Dinner?

What's for dinner? Let's go out tonight. Sounds good, right? We can have a family night out. It will just be us and the three kids. Such a simple idea. Will an inkling of desire leads us to a lovely dinner--or an ill-fated date?

Ahh, food that I didn't make! It's not an impossible dream, it's a delicious one. I don't dream often, but when I do, I dream big!

One mommy, one daddy, and three children embark on an adventure. It's go time. It starts with the chasing and jumping of hoops. Again, with the chasing.

Mom Prob: If I didn't have kids I would probably never run.

You can set up booby traps around the house to snag the little escapees. Just remember where you laid your traps otherwise you might be the one who gets snagged.

Child the first gets dressed while we track down our other two children.

The second child never wants to leave, at first. We have to entice him with something. After he is convinced that dinner will be had, he is on board. A bit over eager at this point, but at least he is on board. Stop shoving your shoes in my face, boy.

He is now running about exclaiming he is Superman. Although I do believe if he were Superman, finding his clothing, not to mention the action of dressing, would not be a problem. Superman would be dressed and fed in less time than it takes this rascal to claim the impossible. Still, as long as he is game, so are we. We get him dressed.

Now we enlist the man-to-man defense, which is using child one to entertain child two. This mainly means making sure he doesn't de-clothe mid-prep. While they run about screaming and mothering (no, they are not one in the same! There's an *and* there) one another, we move on to number 3.

He doesn't care one way or the other what we tell him, mainly due to his inability to understand the English language, or any language for that matter. The details of dinner do not matter to him either. He can drink his dinner in reverse downward dog while kicking his feet at the side of his crib and pulling the curtains off the wall. We frantically get him bathed, slathered in lotion, and clothed.

During what we call the 'finding' stage, we take turns switching off and on between self-prep and kid-prep. We must gather all of Grunt's necessary equipment, which includes: two prepared bottles, extra bottle ingredients, one dish-worth of a meal, and snacks. The boy likes to eat, even if he doesn't get excited about it. Don't forget his toys, which are mainly used for throwing at my face; they are necessities nonetheless. You can't put a price on good entertainment.

We are like a team of NBA players, floating in and out of rooms, hair flying behind us, a look of pure determination on our faces. As we pass each other, items are tossed to whoever is searching feverishly for them. I can't lie. I've caught a shoe to the face a time or two. You just kind of have to go with it. On the other hand, you can do the ol' basketball flop, but that tends to be counterproductive. Whack. Hang on, can only see from one eye....er..ah.

If I'm lucky, I'll have a chance to tame my hair and put on a smudge of makeup. This happens about one out of four times, so the odds are against me getting that one. If I am really on the ball, I even have a chance to check myself in the mirror.

Asking the Man how I look is out of the question. I'll never live down that hole in the jeans I wore all over town that ONE time. Although I still stand by the claim that it was his fault since he was my outfit inspector that evening. Clothing malfunctions are a no, and all of the kids are presentable, at least for the moment. Having presentable kids is a major accomplishment. But it's like building a sandcastle. Quick! Give yourself a mental high-five, since it never lasts.

We head to the car and start the tedium of buckling. Hands are crisscrossing. Kids are crying from the boredom of waiting. I know how you feel, kid. It was only two hours ago that we decided to go out. It's too late to turn back now. If Frodo can make his arduous trek to Mount Doom, then we can make it to dinner. Here we come, Sauron, Lord of the Onion Rings.

Buckled, buckled, buckled, buckled, and buckled. How many kids do we have? I keep losing track. We start the car and the whining begins. Not the car. The kids. Why did we bring them with us again?

"It's hot back here." "Turn the AC on." Number two is kicking my seat and laughing as hard as he can to amuse himself. I, however, am not amused. "Open the sunroof." I return the rapid-fire volley with, "Shut the front door!" No, seriously, the front door was ajar.

Just 10 minutes to get to the restaurant. Only 10 measly minutes and we can eat. "CAN WE DO IT?!!" All together now, "YES WE CAN!!" (Thanks, *Bob the Builder*. Wink, wink. Call me.)

We pull up to the restaurant. By this time, the Grunt has probably fallen asleep. What joy! We now begin the unbuckling phase. Unbuckle, unbuckle, oh, who cares?

We walk in with our cranky, half-awake baby in one set of arms, number two is holding one adult hand, number one is reaching for number two who doesn't want to be touched by his sister, and the 300-pound baby bag packed-- full of things I hardly touch when I have them, but need every time I don't. Funny how that always seems to happen. Must be some untold, mysterious law of the universe.

There is a purse on one arm; another arm is reaching for number one so that number two will calm down about being touched by her. Cranky is waking just enough to register his dislike of this ordeal. Yes, going out to dinner is so much less work than eating at home. Whoever suggested this needs a stern talking to.

Here's where the real fun begins....

We take our seat with the three kids we belong to. We still need a high chair for the smallest who is just now able to sit up on his own.

Mom Prob: Yes, there is a time when they can't even sit up on their own.

How did humans get to be at the top of the evolutionary pyramid?

Asking for a highchair tends to confuse the already confusing situation. So please add another five minutes before we can actually settle in properly.

The best plan of attack is to actually have an idea of what we want to eat before we ever sit down. If we don't have an idea then it is just like adding an atom bomb to a volcano. Yeah, we hadn't planned *that plan of attack.*

I'll let you know right now that even if one of us knows what we want to eat; the odds will never be in our favor.

We try not to look like we are having our first encounter with the civilized world. The idea is to enjoy dinner without having too many bathroom breaks, sibling eruptions or baby meltdowns. Sometimes the idea remains just that.

From the perspective of the random observer, our family dinner must look more like a safari attraction. Middle child is climbing around, making indiscernible noises to any person who will look his way. If he makes eye contact, they have made a pet...er....friend for life.

Oldest child is talking and babbling to herself while she colors each minuscule shred of paper in front of her, including child menus, napkins, pretty much anything that was once a tree.

Youngest child-baby is slapping the table as though he were a caveman, purely for research purposes.

As the babbling paper-fiend, and howling monkey-noises increase, so does the repetitive thudding of chunky baby flesh against tabletop. It echoes through the restaurant and boomerangs back to us accompanied by judgmental stares.

The ultimate embarrassment any parent could ever feel in public is hovering over our heads like a helicopter. Of course, that's noisy, too. We smile boldly back at all those piercing eyes staring them down...because we like to live on the edge...and we look like we do, too.

Our poor server has been able to squeak out our requests and (hopefully) put our orders into the kitchen. We hunker down as our internal hunger clocks tick in unison with our unsettling herd noises. Moo.

We shush, and calm, and dig down into the very crevices of each and every one of our bags looking for food (yes, food), entertainment, and something to soothe the restless. I can feel a frantic mess showing on my face as incessant noise and hunger grates on me.

Somehow, Daddy is oblivious to the utter bedlam fluttering around our empty plates. I sit and yank number two down from yet another precarious position. Number one is handed more paper and an extra pen because apparently the first two pens did not have enough ink. Number three is cooed and held until an arm goes numb, then it's time to switch arms, only to have to switch again under the weight of our beloved Chunka Kahn (The kid has a lot of names).

Our eyes burn holes into that kitchen door. We pray for food (or some sign of it) like we've never prayed before. Hunger isn't even a concern at this point. We just need something to appease these beasts before they resort to cannibalism. I don't even care about the noise anymore. I am so hungry at this point that I sympathize with Anthony Hopkins and think about ordering a nice bottle of Chianti.

The food finally arrives. That was the longest 15 minutes of our lives. Whew. Food! We arrange the plates in front of one and two and begin to relax. Ha!

Kid the first goes to town. She will eat an entire $85 bowl of macaroni and cheese in less time than it would take her to count to three while jumping rope and chewing gum. Don't try to understand. It's fast. Done.

Kid the second is another story. He likes rice. If he cannot get rice then he will accept French fries. No French fries, then give him some pie. If the availability of rhyming food is not going to happen, then we have no choice but to resort to bribes and threats. We will not reprimand the boy in public. He knows this. Big mistake. Once again, do not let children know parent secrets. Once they do, your illusion of control becomes trans*parent*. This is why the United States government has so many different agencies. Protect those secrets!

We resort to threatening him with an early bedtime because he knows he can laugh in the face of public spankings. But oftentimes his laugh only makes us laugh, and then we've blown any chance of coming to an 'agreement' with the boy. So what do we do? Laugh about it, of course.

> **Mom Prob:** Do not let them work out your secrets.
>
> *Switch things up to keep the upper hand. Make them question your every move so that you can confuse them into submission. This is one of the most important lessons you will learn in Parenting 101.*

Mom and Dad desperately want to eat. This is where child the third comes into play. Until recently, he wasn't able to actually eat food. His current appetite reflects his fear that we will start withholding again. When he realizes there is food to be eaten, he goes into overload mode, grunting 'all the way, HA, HA, HA!!'

Once the feeding frenzy begins, it does not stop until he is satiated. And neither does the grunting, with the exception of an occasional grunt of satisfaction afterwards. Hey, it's not for nothing that we wonder about him being part you-know-what.

The sensible thing would have been to have his meal ready ahead of time. Oh, that's right, this isn't McDonald's. Or we could have timed it so that...hey, hold on. I am planning a meal here! The whole point of going out so I wouldn't have to do that. We'll just have to endure this meal melee and the mess that comes along with it.

We swiftly shovel (forks aren't efficient) food in his mouth. Let's be honest, we really just palm the food into his mouth. We want to enjoy our food before it dries up and flies away. To do that we must attempt the impossible.

We contort ourselves into baby-feeding/self-feeding yogis. One arm is crossed into the mouth of the grunting mule. The other arm is wobbling into our own mouths. Another arm is smacking haphazardly at number two just to keep his overactive butt in check. Where did that third arm come from? Meh. I give up.

Finally, we finish. What are the casualties? Two half eaten adult meals; one fully eaten child's meal (plate literally licked clean); one picked over child's meal; one food-stained Mommy, which includes potato hair and steak sauce eyewear; one irritated and cranky Daddy, who finally opened his eyes to what was going on around him and is now scavenging food left on nearby plates; one red-faced belly-full baby, two happy clueless children, and a half asleep infant.

Perhaps those things don't add up, but who's counting? Don't count them, please. Our babies are fed. Our bags are empty. Our bellies are not full. We are ready to leave.

Time to wave down the server in an attempt to exit with some semblance of dignity. It's a shove-the-money-in-her-hand-without-even-seeing-the-bill kind of check for us. We tip generously considering the way we decimated the place and we gather our 10 tons of belongings for our long journey home.

Upon arriving home we have a snack. I really don't have an explanation for any of that.

Dinner and a Show

Daddy has been working out of town for the past few weeks, which means I'm like a single mom. All single parents deserve awards. Bless your hearts.

Since Daddy was away, I thought I would take the kids out for a treat. What a treat it was.

I took the kids to their favorite place to eat, the Purple Cow. It's a 50's-style diner decorated with purple cows. The kids like it because they get crayons and big sheets to color with cows in unusual settings, you know, acting like humans in human situations. Out of 60 plus crayons, they always end up arguing over one purple crayon. Oh, well.

After having been seated for about four minutes my second child tells me that he needs to go 'powwee.' That's potty for those of you who don't understand his age-related 'speech impediment.' Potty, oh joy. I thought, 'Hey, I can do this. It will only take a minute or two.'

I tell my daughter to sit with Mister Grunty, detailing her plan of action, including bullet points. She nods in agreement that she understands. I gather Ding-Ding up as he is doing his yellow rain dance.

The bathroom buddy and I dash away. As I pass the men's room and head for the ladies', my wiggling wee-wee maker points out that we are going in the wrong room. I say, "uh, huh" and continue through the door with the insinuative female form on it. I'm assuming the triangular figure is a woman, because women are the only ones who wear dresses, right? It's not like my son has ever put on a skirt and danced around the house. Although, now that I think about it... there are very few things he hasn't worn while dancing around.

It takes us no time to answer nature's call. We head over to the sink. Soap! As soon as he sees it he realizes his need to bathe in it. Liquid soap is pouring down on him as if it were ambrosia from the Gods. The curdled pink ooze is flowing out of that plastic box prompting me to ask myself, 'Who am I'm gonna call?'

No, child, we do not have time for this. Puppy eyes are being made (by me) and water is splashing like Niagara Falls. I grab three rolls of Brillo brand paper towels and begin dabbing. 'What was I doing in here in the first place?' After a total of two minutes in the 'fun room' we wrap it up. The din of the hand dryer has kept me from hearing what lies beyond the door.

Screaming. The kind of screaming that echoes off windows and shatters glasses. I feel my face warming (and I can only imagine turning bright pink) with embarrassment as I recognize the screams in (no) question. Frantically I start yanking my beloved bubble-boy in the direction of my shrieking scene-maker.

As I round the corner, I see him surrounded by five waitresses. Only he is not having *any* of what *they* are serving. Tears are streaming down his beet-colored cheeks. His mouth is awkwardly contorted from fury. These ladies are oohing and aahhhing over him while he just wails away.

What is my daughter doing, you ask? Why, she is coloring her purple cow in absolute serenity. The child is oblivious to all of the above. So much for the detailed instructions I had just given her. Perhaps I should have written them down.... with that <u>purple</u> crayon. Note to self for future reference.

Mom Prob: The things that seem important to grown-ups are not always important to kids.

Do your best to remember this when you set your expectations.

Rushing toward the table, I'm already making my apologies. I throw out a few thank yous while trying my best not to look anyone directly in the eyes. I imagine a scarlet B emblazoned across my shirt. Today's letter (B) is brought to you by this Bad Mother. They walk off, looking back with sympathy (I hope) as I am still assessing my massive error in judgment.

I grab the Grunt, attempting to calm him the best I can; he always prefers his father when he is upset, and well, Daddy isn't here now is he?

I explain the intricacies of bathrooms, little boys who need to go, and mommies in the most sing songy animated character voice I have. FAIL. I try to convince him that I would never actually leave him. He glares at me in disbelief. FAIL. I'm hugging and consoling him like the baby I still wish he was. FAIL. Nope, it's not calming him. In fact, I think it is actually making it worse. FAIL, FAIL, FAIL!

Finally, I confess that I am a horrible mother, which, oddly enough, calms him right down. As I'm sitting in quiet contemplation, keeping my head down, the world around me sloooowly returns to normal. To think I only wanted to do something different with the kids. Boy, did I ever.

After things settled, the ireful innocent proceeded to make the largest mess I've ever seen and it was all directed at me. He chucked what edibles he hadn't eaten at his thoughtless Mommy, continuing his tirade by attempting to devour the table, high chair, and its belt.

I sat simmering in Grunt's dinner and became painfully aware of how much more difficult life could be. Strangely, in that moment I felt thankful. That ideation was immediately trailed by another thought, 'Never again.' As the words popped through my addled brain, I smiled-- just like I'd rehearsed so many times before.

Kidology

Move it or Chews It

I officially have a crawler in my house. He is a mobile tyrant who knows no limits! The Grunt is a headstrong, face-first, full-on mess whose ultimate plan is to be overlord of his house.

Warning: Crawling is a precarious mode of transportation, especially in a house with siblings.

Obstacles abound. Child locks are fully engaged, he has had to outmaneuver them and us in order to force his will upon us.

Matchbox cars clone themselves over time. I swear, I only remember having ever bought one. Now hundreds of these miniscule motor vehicles line our hallway like a highway at rush hour. Transformers await in the nooks and crannies of each room, ready to crash down on the head of an unsuspecting victim.

This wonderland for creeping babies is a nightmare for a person with OCD--just one more reason to tear my hair out. (I'm surprised I have any left.)

The plants in my house have created a forbidden jungle that Alexander the Grunt simply cannot allow to grow or go untouched. Their irresistible emerald leaves beckon him. He creeps up examining them with an innocent awe and wonder and then goes in for the kill!

He has mastered the intact root pull, rivalling the technique of the best master gardeners. It's like magic, similar to pulling the tablecloth out from under dishes without disturbing a single item. I am still in negotiations with him to show me his secret.

My empty pots sit there, sadly, as the ferociously grinning baby giant hovers over them. Once he discerns that his unearthed treasure is unfit for consumption, he immediately tosses his defenseless find aside like the Babyzilla he is. As I sternly call out his name, he looks at me with the pride of a game angler who just caught the 200-pound prize winning fish.

I am aware that I should be quite upset, but he is so proud of himself and he's so darn adorable. My shock quickly dissipates with a mildly amused laugh and a smile of surrender. I decide he can continue yanking out the plants, as long as he does it with one swift tug. It's easy enough for Mom to stick them back in the pots since the roots are intact. You've got to pick your battles, right?

This Gruntzilla is now a master mover who must have been born with forbidden object homing devices implanted in his feet. They hone in on everything that he is not allowed to have. My main method of deterrence is to move him to the farthest point away from whatever it is he is gunning for.

I grab the kid by any body part I can, charge across the room, baby extended in front of me, place him on the floor, then turn and run with the speed of fright back to the other side of the room. I have to make it back before he does. The idea is to give myself a small advantage where I can get whatever he is after, put away before he attempts to devour it.

Much of my day is spent keeping a step ahead of him, moving him from one part of the room to the other and stashing things out of his path of destruction. You would think that since I am three times his size, I would have the leg up, but you are forgetting that he has two legs up on me and all four limbs going for him. It's a close race every time.

It's like a never-ending game of chess, in which I am always his pawn. We shuffle about from room to room until the house is finally 'clean' enough for the Grunt to scuttle around and scavenge for his favorite 'foods,' you know, like table legs, carpet pads, laundry, which is mostly clean. Only the best for child number 3!

Grunt is not the most graceful of babies and he makes no effort to be either. Like an alpha gorilla, his thighs pound the floor with intimidation and might. His vast jungle consists of plants, toys, and household items. If he realizes that we are sabotaging his efforts to rule, he will push us out of his way and beat on our heads, feet, or any body part he can reach in a display of dominance. If we do not yield to his might, he then resorts to chewing on our extremities.

This is a threat that is not to be taken lightly. His teeth are sharper than any you have ever encountered (except maybe a shark's tooth--or perhaps a piranha--or...). Those 'delicate' baby teeth are constantly gnawing on furniture, fallen limbs, bricks, and anything that will sharpen those tiny pearly whites.

He once showed me his might with his biting prowess. Brace yourself--this next story is not for the faint of heart. While watching TV, my attention was momentarily diverted, read: not 100% focused on Grunt. Evidently, that was unacceptable. All at once, I felt this warm, wet blob attach itself to my forearm. Before I had a chance to evaluate the seriousness of my situation, he had sunk his teeth into my flesh.

Out of reflex, for a split second, I flailed my arm with child attached attempting to release the alligator-like-lock his jaws had on me. I stopped short of chucking the little monster against the wall, but not before I terrified him with my sudden reaction and blood curdling screams.

Our situation changed just as quickly as it began. Rather than tending to my seriously injured arm, I swallowed the pain to cuddle and comfort my wild animal of a child. The perpetrator was consoled by the victim. Sometimes this parenting thing makes no sense. Still, the lesson I learned from my baby is that maternal instinct eclipses all, when it comes to your children.

The Mystery of the Black Eye Culprit

Sometimes I have a difficult time getting a straight answer out of Ding-Ding. He can mix up details, leave some out, or even just concoct entire stories all together. Traversing the language barrier also requires a soft touch. Let's see how I handle this incident.

Yesterday, my son came up to me with a black eye. He insisted that his sister had hit him in the face. He was very upset and I could tell he wanted her to be punished for what she had done. His sister is not a mean-spirited child at all. So I thought that perhaps it was an accident. She is an extremely clumsy girl, so accidents happen A LOT in our house.

They had been playing Mario on the Wii earlier and I thought maybe she had gotten a little out of hand using the controller. She adheres to the karate style video game technique- the full gamer workout. She literally jumps over treacherous turtles, gallops past the goofy goombas, and barrels under birdos. Mario hasn't got anything on Kiki.

I put on my investigating glasses (they're like regular glasses only clean) and went to work. I wanted to see if it was all just an accident of Mario proportions.

When I asked her, she said she hadn't hit him at all. I was bewildered, but I believed her. I tried to interrogate the victim again to get a few more details since the stories weren't matching up.

I asked the 3-year-old to tell me once more how he obtained his ocular discoloration. He kept referring me to his sister. She kept denying the incident involved her at all. I started to experience a touch of vertigo as I questioned back and forth. I was perplexed and horrified about the bruise that was going to be stamped on my boy's face for the next few days.

Oftentimes, in Mommy world, two stories conflict and you just have to see if they will play out on their own. We let the matter settle a bit and decided to revisit it at a later time. Kids have short attention spans, and I thought maybe we could have a little 'caught in the act' later on. Desperate times, my friend.

That night, we were sitting in the living room watching a cartoon. The boy once again started accusing his sister of hitting him. As he was blaming her for his eye, he balled his little fist up and proceeded to smack himself in the face as hard as he could. He then began to laugh and rock back and forth in his chair as we all sat there stunned in shock. It was like something out of a movie. A very disturbing documentary perhaps?

Outraged by what 'she' had just done he cried, "See, Kiki hit me!," Whoa, wild child, slow down now. We just watched you beat yourself up. Yet, you are still trying to blame the girl? I am not sure if that was genius or... no, no it was not. I'm beginning to question EVERYTHING.

As parenting days go this was not one of my favorites. I have two problems now: a son who has started lying, and a son who is using blunt force against himself. I am not sure what's worse. Like I said, I am questioning everything.

Spontaneous Combustion

When new parents talk about how hard it is to have one baby, I laugh. Admittedly, I too once thought that having one child was difficult. It makes me nostalgic for those quiet moments that I once took for granted. My daughter has always been a joy, but every child is capable of shocking you at any moment. I honestly believe kids are here to test our fortitude. Don't let those darling little faces fool you. Let me show you what I mean.

We had moved to a new city and were settling into our apartment. It was a spacious two bedroom, two bath situated on a beautiful lake. (I know I should go into real estate.) In short, we were super ecstatic about this move.

We decided to reward ourselves. We were going to have cable TV for the first time in years. I know that seems hard to believe for some of you TV-tethered parents. Now, it's not that we were hippies, and frankly, I dig hippies (but it's doubtful my constant state of stress would 'Zen' well with their way of life).

We were the ones who always bought movies the second they were released--from the stock boy's grip. We chose not to have network channels jammed into our already crammed lives.

Not wanting to overcompensate by going the cableganza route, we settled on the two-room special for the living room and our bedroom. It was a way for us to spend time together, but apart.

After a full day of unpacking, we let our daughter watch television in our room. She was enthralled. She was overjoyed. She was lost to us. I could quite literally yell "COOKIE" two inches from her face and she would be oblivious. It was both amazing and frightening.

I was envious of the hold this magic tube had over her sweet innocent little mind. Oh, to possess magical powers such as these!

Kiki and her troop of stuffed primates were piled up on her parent's bed watching *Dora the Explorer*, allowing mom and dad a little adult time. Don't get any ideas! Adult as in without a child wedged between us. I won't lie though (and I'm not proud of it) I felt a slight spring of happiness because all of a sudden we miraculously had a toddler-quieting device.

I felt guilt along with my gratitude and thought maybe we hadn't made such a horrible choice after all....maybe...

There she was surrounded by pillows and 20 of her closest stuffed animal friends. She was the absolute picture of contentment. We gave her a time limit, so as not to overdo the brain numbing. Then I backed slowly out of the room, taking care not to set off the parent motion detector. She didn't flinch.

I paused to take a mental picture of my doll among the dolls. She was so happy, independent of Mommy and Daddy. It was like a little rite of passage and I never wanted to forget it. She remained glued to the TV monitor.

Not long after, the man who eats my food and I started smelling something a little unusual. We looked at each other casually as we tried to sniff inconspicuously, you know, spy sniffing. We didn't want the other to think we were attempting to smell what we were sure the other had caused. We've all been there.

We soon realized that we had caught a whiff of something that was more than a little off. After our nose squinching verified we were both in sniffing mode, we dared speak aloud about the offensive matter at hand.

My husband and I paced the hallway, noses upturned like hound dogs. We immediately checked on our little love; still enfolded within her fortress of furry friends. Nothing amiss there, so we began nosing around for other possibilities. A full nasal investigation was underway.

I went out the front door--nothing foul there. I wondered if a fish had flipped up 30 feet out of the water, landed on our terrace and was searing in the heat of the sun. (Hey, stranger things have happened. Have you looked at Reddit lately?) Nope, no fish flopping fiascoes there.

Puzzled, we continued sniffing around for a few minutes before finally resuming our TV viewing. The smell was intensifying and it wasn't my husband's old sneakers. We were not imagining things. We rushed back to the scene of the serene princess, still in bed. This time I yanked open the master bath door only to be hit with a wall of blue and orange tinged smoke!

Smoke was rolling out of our plastic Tri-Wizard goblet and all manner of toiletries were melting and burning into one another. Our wastebasket was on fire. Spent toilet paper rolls were fueling the magical blaze. As I stood totally petrified, the quick thinking man pushed me out of the way to squelch the furious flames. I was one impressed Muggle.

I turned toward my daughter whose eyes remained undiverted from Dora dancing across the screen with the naked boot-wearing monkey. "Yay! We did it, we did it. Hooray!" It was as if they were mocking me with their song of accomplishment.

My daughter never budged, not the first or second time her crazed parents (both of whom thought the other had previously checked the bathroom) came into the room, or when they went rushing out with a fire-breathing trashcan. She was mesmerized into a state of bliss by stars and lizards that laugh and sing and she hadn't even blinked. Not even the fire snapped her out of it.

Apparently, this exhausted from moving mommy had left a scented wax warmer burning on the bathroom counter. Somehow, the tea light candle had jumped into and ignited the refuse. I, however, refused to believe it had any choice in the matter.

I turned off the cartoon. It took a few seconds for Kiki to detach her focus from the TV. Once I was actually making eye contact with her again, I asked if she had been in the bathroom. She nodded. I asked if she had started a fire. She said no.

Knowing my interrogation was going poorly; I picked up the warmer in question and used makeshift sign language to illustrate my point. She looked at me bewildered, as though I needed a flat screen surrounding my face to merit her attention. After a long thoughtful pause, she said, "Yes." She then turned her sweet little pyromaniac head right back toward the television, thus indicating that our conversation was over. I stood there in disbelief.

As we sat enthusiastically watching TV in one room, while we assumed our daughter was doing the same in another, she had slipped away from her intense viewing pleasure for a brief moment. She had the concentration to play Firestarter but couldn't direct that focus on me or hear what I was saying?!

Our daughter's curiosity almost caused a calamity. What do we do when we take a pee break? We create an inferno! My child tossed a candle into the wastebasket during a commercial and resumed viewing her regularly scheduled program. It was astounding.

During the 20 minutes we spent frantically looking for the source of the suspicious stench, we not once suspected our child of so much as shifting from her spot. Foolish young parents we were!

I learned two lessons from that all 'too close for comfort' incident.

1. Just because something smells sweet, doesn't mean it stays that way.

2. Dora is a much better explorer than I am-- and so is Kiki!

Mom Prob: How much TV is too much?

The average kid spends about eight hours a day with their little faces in front of a screen--TV, Smart-phones, iPads, tablets, computers, and more. How often do we hand our kids over to technology? These Kid Tips will help to find balance between reality and reality TV.

a. Take cues from your kids. Watch their behavior. Too much TV and they become irritable. They are aggravated with one another more easily and oftentimes will give me attitude as well. Time for a device detox.

b. Get them outside, involved in a game, project or activity that engages their minds as well as their bodies! Children possess unlimited creativity. Their imaginations can take them to more places than cartoons, movies or video

games ever could.
***c.** Creativity. It's a terrible thing to waste. Don't let technology do all the thinking for your children.*

Oh, and if your child is so transfixed on the TV that you are met with no response, then it's safe to say, it's time for said zombie to be parted from hypnotic screen for sure, wouldn't you say?!

The Stages of Eating a...

First, you see this mysterious bright yellow orb. Your heart rate rises with your curiosity. You are the conquistador and this is most certainly your gold.

You squeeze it extra hard once it is in your grasp and it's juices are at your mercy. Your eyes widen with power and greed. You must have it!

Everything looks delicious, but this will be extra delectable. You can sense it. There is something special about it, perhaps the scent.

You investigate it, rolling it around in your hands a bit. Carefully, you bring it to your nose and sniff it generously before truly considering touching it to your mouth. Savor this journey.

Finally, it's time to take that giant leap of faith and take a taste. This thing is bitter and tart to the tongue. Fruity flavors are floating around your perceptively picky palate. This is a sea of unchartered waters and you are being tossed about like a shipwrecked castaway.

It takes you a few seconds to come to any sort of conclusion about this wondrous delectable. You always ponder things of this nature with the greatest of care.

What is this strange yellow thing that you have been given? What is the meaning of this citrine wedge? What is it that I am to do with this acidic inedible thing? Why did the woman who yells Grunt give it to you?

You begin to question your entire existence. What is the purpose of this? Is this but a test? Your tongue is flicking about in lemony sauces as you ponder life and the meaning of lemons. The tartness intensity is a tad too much for your tiny taste buds.

The moral implications associated with this single serving of lemon are weighing on you. You have found your peace with the giver of fruit, but you are now suspicious of all things handed over. You throw her a distrusting look and let her know that she is on your list. As soon as you learn to write a list, she will most definitely be on the top of it.

You have philosophized all things and are quite sure that you now understand everything and nothing all at once. Life is the ultimate mystery, and this lemon is but a tiny seed amidst it all.

You have concluded that, in reality, you know nothing, and to further prove this theory you must once again delve into the depths of misunderstanding. You jump headfirst back into that flavorful fruit to once more and come fruit to taste bud with the unknown.

You are a thinker. You are an adventurer. You live on the edge of a world that is not flat so you have no fear of falling over. Whee!

Nope. You still don't like it. Question it as you may, it won't stop you from repeating this same cycle too many more times to count. Of that, you can be certain.

Chocolate Covered Grunt

Today is my birthday. Again? Again. Apparently they happen every year and there is nothing you can do to stop them. Who knew?

This morning my youngest attempted to bake me a delicious dessert to express his love for me. I had no idea he even knew it was my birthday, or what a birthday was for that matter. Kids sure can surprise you. What he had in store was breathtaking to say the least. Just don't hold your breath while you read this.

The sun was smiling down on me as birds chirped outside. The house was quiet. I thought to myself, 'I must be the only one awake. That's amazing! Maybe I can sneak in a shower before the boys get up.' I jumped out of bed excitedly. Today's gonna be a good day!

I stepped into the hallway, and felt something was off. Perhaps I should say it was on. Something was definitely stuck to the bottom of my foot. There goes my shower. What is this brown powder? I already know that I don't want to know, but I have to know, you know?

My eyes widen. I glance ahead; the trail is coaxing me toward the kitchen. No, I don't want to. Make it stop.

Trepidation filled me as I followed the path that had been carelessly laid before me. I arrived to find the kitchen in a state of absolute disarray. My eyes can only focus on one spot for a split-second before they frantically dart to another disaster area. You know just like you see in horror movies.

The Grunt is wallowing wildly in the middle of a whopping pile of cocoa powder, powdered sugar, and delicate pearl sprinkles. I couldn't even remember how to react as he continued to coat every inch of himself in his confectionary concoction.

Abruptly, I coughed to get his attention. Startled, he jumped up, shaking his head violently. He knows what he did was a big no, no. As soon as his eyes met mine, he flashed a bright smile out from behind his cocoa coated face.

Grunt then proceeded to stick his entire hand in his mouth so he could savor his own flavors. He wasn't the least bit concerned with me intruding on his delicious mishap. I assume it was a mistake, unless of course he was planning on mixing the cake on the floor rather than in a bowl. He then offered his hand for a taste as if to say, "Happy Birthday Mama!" Remember how I suggested you would be tasting the parenting experience? Well, there you go.

If you're ever in a jam, cocoa powder makes a wonderful house deodorizer. Eight hours later and it still smells like a bakery in here.

Mom Prob: Sweets and your little Sweeties.

It's a dilemma every parent faces, to sweet or not to sweet? That is the question. Candy, cake, cookies are all synonymous with children and happiness, but more recently with 'poison.' Healthy eating and food are hot topics right now. Some parents have chosen the all-natural alternative route of agave and coconut oil instead of refined sugar and butter. Many parents can't afford to go completely organic. I, personally, believe that part of being a kid is getting to enjoy a few of those sweet treats. My motto includes these principles:

a. Teach our children WHY we need to eat healthy and then do my best to steer them in that direction.
b. Lead them in the right direction by showing them through example not to overindulge in high sugar treats.
c. Reward them every so often with an indulgent treat--they're kids and it's unlikely that they will avoid it altogether.
d. "Everything in moderation, including moderation" ~ Oscar Wilde

Kids on Display

I took the kids to Chic-Fil-A for lunch the other day. It's one of the only places where they can play and eat simultaneously where we live. The benefit of a play area is that it is a visual incentive for children to eat. You're literally dangling delight in their faces.

They rushed through their lunch as if they were sitting in a fire. Chicken bits were flitting out of their mouths with furious anticipation. Yummy.

They eagerly asked me if they could play. Those almond-shaped eyes looked up at me, demanding only one answer. I nodded slightly in approval, and before I uttered a sound they were gone. The energy they have. If we could bottle it, this country would never be concerned about running out of fuel again.

I watched through the glass like we were at the zoo. Kids on display in their natural habitat. Dozens of feet, arms, hands, and the like collide to form an exciting and never before seen creature. One similar to that of Lovecraft's imaginings of the half-octopus, half-human hybrid. You're enraptured by this amazing mingling of laughter, joy, and creative collaboration.

The Chic-Fi-Cage is a tiny box of a room that's about five feet too small for my tastes. But kids are small themselves, aren't they? So my tiny beasts piled in on top of 10 other kids and went right to screaming and jumping along with them. As soon as I finished my lunch, I grabbed the Grunt and headed in after our pair who was lost among a tangle of limbs.

When I opened the door, a wall of sound whacked me in the face. I immediately recognized it as confusion. Even the Grunt jerked when he heard it. Maybe he was actually lurching toward the action though? He is a kid after all. Here comes the Grunt!

I stepped in cautiously, half-expecting booby traps to pop up. I sat down and immediately lost my ability to think. Try screaming into a glass; it echoes back at you. Here I was, in a fish tank with at least 15 kids screaming louder than the next. At this point, my Mommy Powers couldn't decipher one voice from any other and I couldn't tune in to the sound of my own children.

I shift from side to side hoping to catch a glimpse of one of my kids. I think about how they are dressed to spot the colors they are wearing. Was Ding-Ding wearing a blue shirt today? Maybe it had green on it. Kiki had on jeans, didn't she?

I'm the only parent in here and I'm positive they can sense my fear. A random child steps on another child's face. Have they chucked all of our parental efforts aside and forged their way as wild beasts?

The screaming intensifies. The stepee pushes out from underneath the foot and runs directly to me and says, "They're not playing fair." I squirm a bit more in my seat as I'm now being asked to take control of the situation. There is no fear like that of having to "parent" another parent's child. What do I do? What would you do?

I tell the stepee that they don't have to play with anyone who isn't playing the way they want to. I also explain that I am not the other child's parent and so I cannot tell them what to do. I'm hoping that my answer will quell their need for justice. The stepee looks at me with dissatisfaction and runs away. Whew. I'd rather be a let down, then have to do that again.

Just then, Ding-Ding jumps down the slide and screams for his sister. Good luck with that, boy. She doesn't hear me even when I'm standing right next to her. He's on a Sis-finding quest, but in all the confusion he runs in the opposite direction of where she is and heads up the ladder where he fights a few others to get to the top. This may be a 'Sis-ssion Impossible.'

Kids are jumping in front of each other, barking, laughing like lunatics and running away. They act without rules or regard for the consequences of their actions. Can't help but wonder what the world would be like if adults acted like this. The police would be there in a nanosecond to haul them away in a paddy wagon. It occurs to me that for these little crazies, it is all fun or nothing and it's a good thing they grow into adults. At the same time, I feel like I'm witnessing something spectacular.

Young children accept one another on their most primal level just the way they are, obnoxious, impulsive, outrageous, you name it, they allow it all. They have no expectations, no molds they are trying to force each other into, they just want to be free to explore whatever brings them joy. We could learn a thing or two about simply following our bliss from, you guessed it, our kids. I would recommend reigning it in a bit though.

Kiki

Now we will delve into the mind of a 9-year-old girl. You can look away if it's more than you can handle.

As we sit down across from one another I realize my in be'tween' is nearly the size of the chair she is sitting in. Sometimes I overlook how much she has grown. It is denial, plain and simple. Who wants to see their innocent children grow up? No one wants their children to face a whole wide world of problems. You will always see the baby they once were no matter how old they are.

She already has a look of utter boredom on her face and we've only just begun. I remind her that I am writing a book and ask if she would mind helping me. She agrees. She hasn't shown any real interest in the project aside from the fact that she thinks it's cool she will be in a book.

Her jeans are covered with holes; tattered shredded fabric hangs from her legs casually brushing into the chair. Keeping her clothes intact has been one of my greatest challenges of late. I begin by telling her I will ask her questions that she needs to answer honestly with the first thing that comes into her mind. I let her know that I am going to write down everything she says. She nods, and we begin.

Tell me about yourself.

"I used to have long hair and now I have short hair. I have green eyes. I'm in third grade. I like the show Jessie. I like the color purple. I'm 9 years old. I really like puppies. My favorite holiday is Christmas. I love my family. Done."

She flashes a huge smile and pops up excitedly in her seat as she says, "*Done,*" like she knew every question I was going to ask and answered them all at once. One and done. I let her know that this may take a while and she glances over at the clock and then to the television as if it were desperately calling out for her return. I tell her she can watch TV as soon as we are finished and that it won't take forever.

Kids seem to respond better when the word forever is in play. I don't believe they understand its true meaning, but hey, it works.

My thoughts drift and recall the movie *The Sandlot* before I come back to my own reality. We all need our little escapes. Some more than others. I am a Some.

<u>What would you like to be when you grow up?</u>

"I would like to be a Rock Star."

<u>Why is that what you want to be?</u>

"I just like to sing."

Just the other day she told me she wanted to run a daycare because she likes kids and would enjoy taking care of babies. That same night her Bubba Grunt introduced her to the shocking side of babies by deciding to go naked. His explicit escapades led to him marking his territory, which included her feet. I can still hear her shrieking as he ran for cover. I haven't heard her mention running a daycare since.

I sigh wistfully in my mind. It wasn't that long ago that I had dreams. Now my aspirations consist of taking a nap, and maybe a shower, without being interrupted, if that's not too much to expect.

What advice would you give your kid?

"I would give him or her advice on how to get a job."

She hasn't even had her kid yet, and she already wants them to find a job! I have a feeling she is going to be a wonderful parent!

What would you say about that?

"About like how to get the money from the job. If they asked me if they had to pay to get a job, then I would say, 'No they don't have to.' I would tell them that they have to call the place. If they didn't need them then they would have to get another job somewhere else."

Wise beyond her years.

What is the best job?

"A job that is a little bit easy for them and that they can make good money at. The most important thing is that they need to care for their family."

<u>Do you want to be a Mommy?</u>

Just as I get the question out, the Grunt charges in and throws a book across the room. Kiki immediately jumps into action, grabbing him from behind and hugging him across his chest. She scolds him as she pulls him away from his latest demolition site, *"No, Bu-u-bba."* My sweet southern belle can turn any two-syllable word into six with her delightful drawl.

I repeat my question.

<u>Do you want to be a Mommy?</u>

"Yes." She smiles and looks down shyly. As she's attempting to hold Grunt hostage he leaps from her embrace and plows his way back out of the room. She calmly walks over and picks up the mess he couldn't care less about.

Containing my reaction to her answer (both verbal and otherwise), I think to myself that 35 would be a good age for her to start her own family. Yeah, mid-thirties is about right for my little girl.

<u>What do you think that means?</u>

"You have to do hard work."

<u>Like what?</u>

"Like whenever they're first born you have to change their diaper. You have to feed them milk whenever they're born. When they get bigger, you have to tell them to clean up their room. And tell them to brush their hair and teeth when they forget."

How many kids do you want to have?

"One." This is actually the first time she's ever told me how many kids she wants. She's talked about being a mother often, but never indicated how many children.

Why only one?

"Because it would be easier. Because you wouldn't have to talk to them all at once and they wouldn't have to talk to you all at once."

I find it interesting that she has already learned the rule of one, a rule I clearly didn't know! Kids are a lot smarter than we think they are, sometimes smarter than adults are. Don't ever admit this to a kid though. We adults must uphold the illusion of superiority!

What would you name your kid?

"Um, if it was a boy he would be named Zane."

What made you think of that name?

"I just heard it. If it was a girl I would name her Shell."

Where did you hear that name?

"It was on my Monkey's tag."

Monkey is one of her stuffed animals. She went through a phase and amassed quite the collection of stuffed primates. Among them is a one-armed Gorilla named Gary, a red Orangutan (yet to be named) that takes sabbaticals for weeks at a time, we have a tie-dyed Chimpanzee named Pip, a Bonobo named Bon-Bon, and a rag-tag troop of various unnamed primates. She has a zoo-full of stuffed animals. I'm just relieved I don't have to feed them. That would drive me bananas.

If your kid did something bad, what would you do?

"Um, I would tell them to think about what they did. I would tell them to try and think about something they could've done instead of that."

That's straight out of the Reece handbook right there.
I'll take that as a win.
Kids-32,537,632, Mom- A whole lot less.

MOMent: When your kid realizes you actually do know a few things and that sometimes you can do something right.

They only help to reinforce your parental esteem. Thanks kid, for letting me know I've done well! Relish these moments. They are rare.

What do you think the best thing about being a parent would be?

"To spend time with your child and having fun. Maybe going on a vacation with them. We could go to the Farmer's Market."

Is that the best thing about being a parent?

"One of them. Another best part is getting new stuff that we all like."

I like stuff. Who doesn't like stuff?

Stuff, like what?

"Like getting new furniture that we all would like."

I'm not sure that's the stuff I was previously thinking about. I guess there's nothing quite like bringing home a credenza for the kids!

What fun things would you do with your kids?

Grunt barrels through the room clenching his teeth and a small toy. Ding-Ding clumsily chases after him. The troublesome twosome crash into everything as they run in circles around the living room. Apparently the mighty titan has taken possession of a highly coveted object and Ding-Ding is in hot pursuit.

Kiki sighs heavily as they continue their never-ending game of cat and mouse. Poor firstborn can't ever get a moment. She answers me back loudly, doing her best to be heard over the rest of our brood.

"Go to Disney on Ice one day. One day go to their favorite restaurant. Take them to the store and buy them some new clothes." She lets out another sigh. Then turns to me and says, "They're so rowdy," then she glares over at the boys.

Who would have thought that simply speaking could turn into this much work? Every parent ever. That's who. If only we could be transported to some tranquil far off planet. Kiki, beam us up.

What is the best thing about your Mom?

"The best thing about you is, um, you get us new stuff. You take us to fun places. You make our rooms nice. You make a wonderful dinner. You get us new movies. You are nice to everyone. You are giving."

Again with the stuff. Also, you have all just witnessed that I make wonderful dinners (which my kids ALWAYS eat) and I am nice to EVERYONE. End of discussion.

What is the best thing about your Dad?

"He's funny. He likes to sneak candy to his kids. He's also kind of giving. He likes to be nice to you. He always looks out for the kids. Most of the time, he helps out. Except for when he leaves his stuff around. He's dorky and that's funny."

She is right; he's our dork and that makes him a special kind of funny.

What is the worst thing about your Mom?

She immediately looks at her feet and hesitates. I can see she doesn't want to say anything that might be hurtful. I explain to her that I know that I can always do better as a Mommy and that the best way for me to learn is if she can talk to me. I also let her know that she isn't going to get in trouble for telling me how she feels. We are all people and we all have a right to our feelings.

"I don't like it when you get mad at my brother and you make him sad. That makes me sad too. Sometimes I don't like it when you're mad."

Judge me. I totally deserve it.

<u>Why do you think I get mad?</u>

"Because sometimes we do bad things."

<u>Do you think there is a better way I could react when you do something bad?</u>

"Not really. I'm speechless about that."

Why can't she be speechless when I want her to be?

I'll admit I might have been looking for more of a creative solution here. Now I need to switch things up before this interview dies a sudden death.

<u>What is the worst thing about your Dad?</u>

"I knew there was something about that!"

She exclaims as she jumps up in the chair. Bravo child you have figured me out. She isn't hesitant this time. She just starts right in now that she knows she can be honest since he is not there. I may regret this...

"The worst thing is he also gets mad. Also, um, sometimes he makes you mad. And....um.....speechless. Ha!"

He makes me mad, because that's what men do, honey. And, it's a mom's role to annoy daddy. Not intentionally, of course, it's just a law of nature. One day you will understand. Why do you think I want you to put off starting a family for as long as it is biologically possible, child!?

Tell me a funny story about a time with your family.

"When it was Daevyn's first birthday he got a Spiderman cake. We went to Nini's house to celebrate. He had some nice clothes on. We gave him the cake. It was black and red and looked tasty. Daevyn got red and black icing all over him. We then had to put him in the white bath tub at Nini's house. He made a big mess in the tub. It was a little bit hard to get it off of him and the tub."

Why do you think that was funny?

"Because he got it all over him and looked like he painted icing on his face. He was really messy, but he was covered in yummy stuff too!"

It's the little things.

What's the grossest thing you or your brothers have ever done?

"I don't really know anything about that. Maybe when they try to eat dirt."

I'm sure she could have come up with countless stories if she had tried. I am thankful. You should be too. Trust me on this one.

Do you think this is boring?

"Kind of boring. Is that one of the questions?"

Yes, I am boring. I will hold my tears until the end. I hope. Sniff, sniff.

Now it is.

"Seriously?"

What do you think is most important for a mom or dad to be?

"I think that parents need to have love for their children. They need to make sure that they don't just give them everything they want. They also need to have a perfect job."

Children are amazing. Wouldn't you agree?

When you have kids what do you think they will need the most?

"They will need a home the most."

What do you love most about your brothers?

"I love Alexander because he is cute. Daevyn is because he is playful."

I don't want to shatter her illusion by revealing that one day those boys are going to outgrow their cute playfulness. Heck, I wish I didn't have to know the truth either. Is there a way for me to unknow it? Please?

What do you least like?

"I don't like that Daevyn can sometimes be mean and I don't like it when Alexander throws a fit."

I concur. Boys are born to harass one another. It amazes me. I've seen the Grunt sit on Ding-Dings back and jump up and down as if he was riding a whining stallion.

What would you tell your kids about you (right now)?

"I would tell them about my family. I would tell them that I was giving. I would tell them that I had my own room. Speechless."

Speechless again? She's just a sweet chatty girl, and I can't get enough of her.

MOMent: When I have been in a deep conversation with my daughter, only to realize that she had tuned out by my second sentence.

There is a lot to be learned from really listening when your child is talking. When Kiki told me that she sat with a younger boy on the bus and helped him read a book, she was really telling me that she has a desire to reach out and help others, that she has a kind heart and she is full of love and charity. What our children tell us speaks volumes about who they are and who they can be. It is our job to help them become their best selves. Listening is just one of the many ways we parents can gain wisdom from our children.

What is the one thing you want the most?

"To fly. That's pretty much what a lot of people want."

Can't disagree here, although I must say I've always been fond of the idea of teleporting. No more traveling back and forth to the grocery store or long car rides with three cranky kids for this lady. To be perfectly honest, I would SO abuse teleporting. Oh, you need me to reach the remote that is one foot away? Poof, here ya go. Awesome.

Why do you want that?

"Because if I could fly then I could see everywhere. I could see up on everything and I could go there. I could see new people and help them."

I hear helping again. So proud of her. She would obviously be a much better Superhero than her remote teleporting mother.

<u>What would you change about your Mom/Dad if you HAD to change something?</u>

"*Mmmmm. Um, change something,* (as she slouches in the chair and taps softly on her chest, with her feet stretching back and forth rubbing against the carpet,) *I don't know anything.*" She starts bending her hands and arms like she's doing the robot dance. Sits up straight and stares at me like she's ready to get this over with.

<u>What kind of food would you make for your kids? Recipes?</u>

Excitedly, she jumps up. "*I would make, um.*" She's walking around the room scratching her head. "*Rice, macaroni, orange juice for a drink, and the sliced up* (makes a slicing motion with her hand and forearm) *carrots that look like a circle.*"

<u>Tell me anything else that you want to say.</u>

"*You have plants. Daevyn likes dinosaurs. Alexander and Daddy like music. I like reading. We all like spending time together. And you should too!*"

I ask her what 'who' she means by 'you' and she lets me know she means whomever reads the book is the 'you.' Don't let the girl down! Pressure! Feel the pressure!

The Case of the Missing Spider-Man

For more than a month, my 3-year-old man desperately needed new shoes. My mommy brain could not recall this necessity when I was in a store that had little boy shoes. You'd think it would have been a top priority, but somehow it was filed in the cold cases in my head. Curse those nursery rhymes for slowly pushing all those scientific equations into oblivion.

I finally set out to provide shoes (geeze, just another essential, right?) for my son and was met face to face with an imposing pair of Spider-Man sneakers. It was as if Spider-Man himself had web slung them right into my line of sight. It was meant to be. I just knew the boy would jump for joy (and probably smash his head on the floor on the way down) from his overflowing excitement. He does that at times.

I tossed the shoes happily into my cart and caught myself whistling a cheery tune. I can't lie. I was a proud mom.

MOMent: When you know you've done something they are going to adore you for.

Checking this necessity off my list was going to earn me a gleeful squeal from my little cave man. He would be averting danger in style soon enough.

I Yoda'ed the loaded...wait, these are not the words I am looking for... Loaded the Yoda (ah, that's better) full of my acquisitions and headed home, Spider-Man shoes in toe. Yes, pun intended.

The moment I got home, I began unloading the groceries from the many bags I brought in. The recipient of the surprise, not unlike Spider-Man, sensed that there was something to be uncovered. Spider-Man waits for no one and must have been secretly sending signals, because Ding-Ding zeroed in and found those shoes like they had a locator ding coming from them.

He yanked those shoes out of their plastic-bag sheath with such force and purpose that it reminded me of sweet little Wart pulling the sword from the stone. Light beamed down onto him from our ceiling and as I followed the ray up in momentary wonder, I saw that I had once more forgotten to buy a replacement bulb for a nearby light that had burnt-out long, long ago. Aargh!

We now return to our regularly scheduled joy. Pure toddler ecstasy! I had accomplished my mission with 100 percent success. I was excited, which obviously doesn't happen often enough. It doesn't take much to excite me these days. Calm yourselves, I'm not *that* easily excited!

Ding-Ding, of course, had to wear the shoes that very second. Forget the Fritos. Hold off on the hot dogs. Never mind the melting ice cream. For once, a few of his favorite things were no contest for this little man's new shoes!

When Spider-Man calls, you answer and if you are using Spidey Sense—you answer *before* it rings. He put those shoes on before his clothes were even a thought. I kept telling myself it's just a phase, but I'm beginning to think that males just wanna be free—especially of clothes. He stood there in all his glory, like a monkey with no shame.

Suddenly, he became the master of Spider-Man and no villain would go unpunished. He ran around the house springing off the walls like a spider monkey of course, shooting his imaginary webs at his imaginary foes. It was the high point in his entire pro-bono career.

Bedtime came and we were forced to kidnap Spider-Man from the boy's feet. He was heartbroken over the hero's sudden demise. I assured him that Spider-Man would be safely tucked between the old worn out common folk; you know the shoes that didn't shoot the webs and catch the villains.

He went to sleep grudgingly on nothing but promises and hope. He even refused kisses and sleepy time stories. My moment had come and gone. Sigh. I should have known to let him sleep with them in his bed. Hey, why not?

Day 1 came and those shoes were snugly fitted on him like no pull-up ever has been. He ran, romped, and relished every wiggle of every toe in those shoes. No mommy has ever made a more awesome choice in footwear in the history of motherhood. And, judging from the indescribable look of joy on his face, I am confident that there will never be another choice as awesome again.

By lunchtime it was obvious, Spider-Man had taken up permanent residence on those tootsies. The crow bar would have to come out tonight. I would like to add that the boy hated all shoes-- until the day Spider-Man walked through our door.

Day 2 had turned out just as 'Amazing' as the sequel could ever be, or the remake(s) for that matter. Insert Advertisement here.

Day 3 here we go. Ding-Ding was out of bed and pulling at my shirt for me to get his shoes. I went to wake old Spidey from his web, alas; he was nowhere to be found. It was all mommy could do to maintain a calm face through it all.

Mom Prob: Be strategic about your reactions, monitor your reactions, you are the adult they are not.

If you stay calm and act logically, you can keep their emotions from escalating further.

No need to raise suspicion. I made the tactical decision that Ding-Ding needed to play in the bathtub before he put on his underwear and shoes.

You read that right, underwear and shoes, and trust me; just the underwear was a real accomplishment.

While the boy was drowning octopi in the tub, I met with the Flash and decided to have a contest on who could find the elusive Spider-Man first. Blankets were tossed in the air. Toys were hitting walls. Dishes were shuffled about. I went through every pair of shoes looking for that iconic emblem with absolutely no luck.

Apparently, Spider-Man had some epic work to do because he abandoned that boy in the face of insurmountable odds. He must have literally walked right out on us. I felt abandoned. I felt betrayed. More than anything, I felt panicked.

I can't say what he did was right but I CAN say that all we have now is one lonely left Spidey and no accomplice. The right Spidey is a sneaky sneaker.

We have scoured every crack and crevice to no avail. Ding-Ding was right to fear he would leave. I guess I put my faith in the wrong superhero. Next time we will have to go with Batman. You can't go wrong with a billionaire philanthropist, after all. He would never leave a kid without shoes.

Why, oh, why didn't I just let the boy sleep with the Spidey shoes!!??

If you happen across a right foot, Size 8, Spider-Man shoe, you let him know of his epic failure.

There is a boy in the world searching endlessly for him with a mother who is running out of distractions. The search continues...

Momology

Lost and Confound

Losing things is another exciting part of the child-rearing experience. In case you have forgotten, we just lost a one-of-a-kind shoe the other day. That was a bleak day in the Reece household. The Shoe-neral was a somber, yet tasteful affair. Many tears were shed over that lost lonely mate. You might even go so far as to say the *Reeces* fell to *pieces*.

My Mommy brain knew from the beginning that it was a likely outcome. We'll just add it to the heap of misplaced miscellany.

Misplacing objects has become an accepted part of our lives. I have unenthusiastically accepted the fact that our dryer eats articles of clothing. Its appetite has grown over the years. It started out with a sock here and there and slowly grew bolder. I am positive it snacked on a pair of my shorts just last week. I'm plotting my revenge.

Things are always going into 'hiding' in our house. Or maybe they got fed up from the treatment of over exuberant toddler boys and just decided to... disappear. Hopefully, there is a special taskforce assigned to the protection detail of our traumatized missing items. I miss them so much. Maybe I'll see them on a milk carton someday. Sigh.

I think losing my memory falls into this inevitable category of invisibility. Sometimes I wonder if my kids haven't tapped into some sort of magic after all. I'm wondering if they are all tiny Time Lords using TARDISes to shift my belongings and my grasp of reality around.

For me, the craziest part of all of this is that things just randomly reappear. I swear some sort of sorcery is at work. We lost his Spiderman shoe. I literally looked for that shoe every day for more than two weeks. I kid you not. I was bent on finding that shoe and I spent hours in feverish pursuit of it. I eventually gave up. I knew it was illogical, but I had resigned that the shoe had simply walked off.

I told myself it was over and so what did I do? Well, I went out and bought the boy a new pair of those exact Spiderman shoes. That's what we parents do after all. You know this story I'm sure. I bought him a new pair of shoes and three days later, my daughter came out of her room with the missing shoe in hand. Golden hued rays were emanating from her hands as if she was holding the Holy Grail. As the light glinted off of her glorious find I asked her, "Where was that?!"

"It was in my room," she replied. Well, that answers that question doesn't it.

Mom Prob: They will lose any and everything.

Human-like

It's amazing. The first time you hold your first baby you try your hardest to be soft and tender. You are cautious and full of worry. Everything you do is done with the utmost care and thought. There is this protective fear that they will break if you don't handle them like a delicate feather.

Babies are more resilient than you think. They are small and fragile, and yet they are stout and strong. They need so much and are completely reliant upon us, the way the U.S. relies on the Middle East for oil. We need a full tank to best care for them; they themselves are slowly draining our fuel source. They are feeding our coal into their own fires all the while expecting us to do their feedings. Confused? Good. So am I.

Get used to it. That's what happens when you have to wake up every few hours to feed an infant. I remember those days when I would need pliers just to open my eyes. The next morning with my other kids, you can forget me taking the time to lock onto someone's soul. Forget me wielding my mind-control powers to take over another human with nothing more than a glance. Forget me smiling. It is NOT going to happen.

Mom Prob: Having a newborn is hard.

You're welcome.

You move at the speed of a sloth, and fight the almost uncontrollable urge to let your body drift off to sleep on the lost island of Atlantis where you will remain in a sleep trance for as long as you desire.

You pull yourself out of it and up into a human-like stance. Cro-Magnon Man would be proud of how far you have devolved in only a short few weeks. Forget about looking civilized because you know you aren't that got-it-all-together-with-everything-under-control-all-the-time Mom anymore. And at this point surviving is all that matters. Stumbling about in the dark like an ape has shown you the depths of your own humility. And, boy, it's way down there. You begin to wonder if you would even make Darwin's list.

You've held, patted, rocked, bounced, bumped, hummed and swayed yourself to exhaustion, exhausting all means to get him to sleep. All the while, he is lying in your arms wooing you with the most darling song your heart has ever heard and smiling at you ever so sweetly.

You find yourself praising the sleep deities when your baby finally makes it through a single night without waking. While you are doing your sleep dance, you are simultaneously praying that this one night is not a fluke because your drained psyche couldn't bear having this glorious gift returned to sender.

For just a second you forget that you are depleted and frazzled to the core. In a fraction of a second, a paranoid thought flashes, 'He knows what he is doing AND he is laughing at me.' You brush the notion aside as daft. Lack of sleep is simply eating its way through your brain cells. You continue to stumble through your day like a sleepwalking servant to the little master. What day is it anyway?

When you are pregnant, people will tell you to get all of the sleep you can, like you can put it away for a rainy day. There is no such thing as a snooze bank and the person that is able to invent such a thing will pocket every hard-earned dollar that any new parent has. In fact, I have earmarked a small fortune to invest at just the thought of it.

Goodnight My Dear, sweet dreams about sleeping. You shall meet again...one day...so they say.

Put a Lid on it

After nine months of pregnancy, part of you can't wait to return to being a normal woman again. You want to go out and wear clothes that aren't laced with spandex and elastic. You want to step into the world and actually be able to see your feet when you do.

I wanted to get dressed up for absolutely no reason and go out. I didn't really care what I did as long as it involved being in the real world. So about two weeks after having my baby, I decided I would go out and pick up some lunch. It sounds like a simple task doesn't it? You're so silly. I still like you though.

I went to a restaurant and ordered food to take home. Traversing the reality of normalcy had its appeal, but I didn't want to push my outer limits. Plus, I couldn't bear being separated from my newest baby for very long; not to mention I was on a permanent two hour schedule.

After ordering our food, I went over to the self-serve station to get drinks for the family. I feebly pushed my cup against the ice lever and did my best not to fall into the soda machine as I did so. My eyes fluttered a bit as the tiny clear crystallized water cubes dropped melodically into my glass. Who knew this could be so fascinating. Whoops, I pushed the lever a bit too long and ice spilled over the top onto the tray that catches the excess. So that's why that's there!

I looked around quickly to see if anyone noticed. Yep, the man standing right beside me was looking on with disapproval. I can't even fake a smile at this point. Where did he come from anyway? I moved on to the soda section of this trial. Sweet tea, Sprite, Coca-Cola, which do I want? It would be best if I didn't make any tough decisions while in this state of mind, but I have no choice in the matter. Who gave me this assignment? Oh yea, that would be me. Carry on.

Mom Prob: Sometimes it's no one's fault but our own.

While waiting for the order, I fill my cup with my beverage of choice, being extra careful not to let it overflow. I smile to myself, like an idiot. This is an accomplishment? For some strange reason I turn toward the man and grin at him. He remains disapproving. Tough crowd.

I shuffled sideways down the counter to find the lids. Ok, the drink station is here so where are the lids? Lids! I began to panic a bit that someone is playing a cruel joke on me. The man behind me is obviously a spy who was sent to test me on my mission. I just know it. He's a little too interested in my behavior.

Now realize I mean this quite literally, I walked up and down the counter for three minutes. That doesn't sound like it, but it is quite a long time. Try it. It is even longer when you are aware that you are being watched.

Others have joined the man behind me as I have now clogged the soda station with my inability to find those damned lids. While still looking I began to wonder if maybe they are simply out of lids. I looked back to the register for a friendly face to validate this last thought. Nope, and they're all staring at me too. This is a tad bit embarrassing.

Finally, I decided to act like I am getting something else. What can I get? Oh, napkins! I reach for the napkins and step out of the way. As I step aside, the man behind me reaches across me and grabs a lid; he puts it on his cup, and then glances down at my hands holding lid barren cups. Wonder if lidless cups are symbolic of a deep psychological issue?

As he looks me over, I realize something else about myself. I still have bruises on my arms from the hospital IV. I don't mean a tiny speck either. I have a five-inch blue and purple mass surrounding punctures that stretches across the inside of my arms.

My eyes widen and I look up in shock to see my face reflected in the mirror. My hair looks like it could house a family of wrens. It's a massive nest of straw! I have black holes of bags under bloodshot eyes and I was wondering why everyone was staring at me when I looked like I was on *The Walking Dead*. They probably feared for their lives!

Remember that part about me getting dressed up? Yeah, apparently I forgot that part too. I jump back at the sight of myself. Dear lord, who let me escape from the pack of zombies and why? Now everyone in the place is watching my every move. I lunge for those cursed lids as people pull back. I decide not to cause any more of a scene by slinking into the darkest corner to wait for my name to be called. The image of my reflection is burned into my mind as I count the seconds until I can escape this embarrassment.

Finally, my order is ready! I lurch to the counter grabbing wildly at my bags and flee like an escapee. I decided I didn't need to leave the house again for at least a month after that excursion.

Who Me? Couldn't Be

I got a phone call the other day. Impressive, I know. This is how it went.

"Hello, Mrs. Reece?" A female voice was coming from the other end.

"Yes. This is she," me doing my best impersonation of an adult.

"Yes, this is Ms. So and So, the assistant principal." That's not really her name, but wouldn't it have been an interesting one if it were?

Now comes the internal monologue. 'Oh no, what have I done? I am going to be in so much trouble.'

Give me a second. I'm not always the brightest bulb in the shed. Whatever.

'Wait, I'm a grown woman, not a teenager. I'm not in school. I couldn't have done anything wrong. Why is this lady calling me? Oh, wait, something... brain you can do it.

Oh yea, I have a kid! Crap, what did she do?'

Mom Prob: Have you ever forgotten you are an adult?

I have.

Trying not to sound upset, "Oh, Hi. Um, is everything okay?" That whole trying not to sound upset thing didn't really come through like I intended. Please tell me *she* didn't do anything wrong. I don't even know how to Mom right now.

"Oh no! There's nothing wrong I was just calling to remind you about the such and such. I hope you can be there," she said detecting my concern.

"Ok, thanks for reminding me." You've never called before to remind me of anything. I thought I was in trouble and then the kid….and….oy…. act like a Mom. "It was lovely speaking with you," I pause for a second and try to think of something a normal adult would say. "Have a wonderful day." Kissing up I see. Oh, shut it.

"You too, Mrs. Reece. Good Bye." She hung up.

After I put the phone down. I think to myself. 'When did I become an adult, let alone a parent?'

Phony Tails

My daughter's school has what they call Spirit Week. It's that week before Homecoming, where every grade shows their school spirit. Go Team Go! I should've gone into Cheerleading.

Back to my limited skillset. Really, Spirit Week is a week of dressing up in goofy outfits. Each day has a different theme. One was Superhero day. We've had a dress as your favorite Disney character day. There was even a kooky hair and sock day. You get the picture.

The kids like to show off their individuality. It's a chance to make an ordinary week special. Some of the kids really get into it, they'll buy an outfit and spend (what seems like) weeks figuring out the perfect hairstyle.

Then there's my daughter. We'll get an outfit picked out and she begins to tell me how she wants her hair done. That's when it happens…

Her face is full of excitement as her eyes slowly look up locking onto mine. Instantly she realizes who she is talking to and her exuberant smile fades. I do my best to take the matter seriously. "Ok, you want a Chignon. Does that come with grapes?" I am the worst female Mother in the history of the world.

I have very limited womanly skills. Unfortunately, hair didn't make the cut.

All the little girls in her classes always have the cutest hair-dos. My daughter, on the other hand, always looks like she has been chased through a field of hay. We're doing well if her hair is brushed. You want cute, too? 'Fuggeddaboudit!'

So a week of showing off your ability to look cute isn't my idea of fun. I can do 'crazy hair' no problem. Of course, that's just a normal hair-do day for us.

I once tried to practice French braiding on her. We were in the living room watching a movie. She was sitting in between my knees and it looked as if she was practicing for the bobsled. She was probably thinkin', 'Jamaican' me dizzy Mom.' It was making me dizzy just trying to fix it.

By the way, have I mentioned that I'm obsessive? Well, being one who splits hairs but is not predisposed to fixing it is not a good mix. I started braiding; knot one, twist, two. Before her hair was 'braided', the credits were running on the second movie and it still wasn't anything close to 'cute'. Sorry honey.

Boys are much easier. You can slap a tie on them and they're dressed up. Done. Girls, not so much. I've had to learn how to fake the easiest of hairdos. Thus came the phony tail.

After a little of my infamous internestigations (internet investigations for those of you who don't speak Susie) I found the perfect fake-out hairdo device. It's called a 'hair wrapped ponytail.' The inventor must've known about me and my hair-challenged hands.

It's a hair elastic that is covered with fake hair so it looks like you have meticulously and flawlessly (read OC approved) wrapped up your little girls hair when all you really did was make a couple of regular ol' ponytails.

Add a little hairspray. Make that a lot and from a distance, it's the perfect coiffure. Just don't get within a few feet otherwise you meet all the Vidal's and Sassoon's and my trick may be exposed. Instant hero Mom.

I never knew part of the requirement for having a girl was to have a talent with hair. Looks like all the other mothers got that memo though.

Mom Prob: Having girls means having to know how to do hair.

There's Youtube for that.

Sleep it Off

We celebrate all of our kids accomplishments. The first laugh is recorded for all of humanity to witness...until the end of time. Their first food is Page 10 of the sacred baby keepsake journal. Remember kid, no green bean was as special as that first one. Those first steps lead your family to take you on tour. Even your third cousin twice removed somehow merits a visit. We tend to overindulge kids when they learn a new 'trick.'

Well, the smallest of my pack has learned how to get out of bed by himself. Way to go! Right? WRONG!! This is not an accomplishment to be celebrated.

Escaping the cage...I mean, uh, crib opens their world to a slew of possibilities....NONE of which are good. I've gone through this exciting stage before and each time I'm left with the same outcome: discord of the highest order!

You see, when they can escape they are instantly face to face with their free will. No, not Free Willy (but I'm sure he felt the same way when he lept over those rocks). They haven't had free will before now? Yes and no. We parents are the gatekeepers of the elusive Free Will. We can either allow their little hearts to explore without restraint, or we can stop them from eating toilet paper while leaving a trail of it throughout every room in the house. The decision lies in our grown-up hands.

Call it a sixth sense, but kids know that we are the reason they aren't really having all the fun they possibly could. Ideally (for us), the first thing they would do when they finally learn how to get free would be to wake us up. Don't think that is part of their plan.

Imagine you've been in prison and you've just dug your way to freedom. What is the first thing on your to do list? If it's 'find a uniformed guard' you may want to reevaluate your agenda. They've escaped and they really want to take a bite out of freedom, and all the cake and cookies they can find before you stop them!

I'll admit there have been times when I would wake up and realize that my house was being trampled by tiny feet. Fright sprang up in me like a Jack in the Box. I'd start questioning everything. What is that noise? How long have they been awake? Which room are they in?

If I lie here, a while longer maybe I'll really wake up and he will still be asleep. If your house gets wrecked while you're still in bed, they say sleeping it off is about the only thing you can do. Then get up and mess it up some more. Little hair of the dog...

Mom Prob: Sometimes you just have to pretend to be asleep.

Thou Shalt Not Curse

WARNING: If offended by swearing, please skip this next admission. Wouldn't want it to bias you against the rest of this collection of family tales.

This is the one that's supposed to be hush-hush. This is the one thing that could cause some of you to think less of me as a person. It's true; what you are about to read is not reflective of my best moment, but this is a book of lessons and we all learn from our mistakes.

Judge me. Do it. Judge me long and hard, and then I want you to sit back and judge my honesty as well. If you don't want to be critical of me, just go with it because it works better with this intro. Thanks for working with me on this one.

Here it is. I curse. My husband curses. We can swear like drunken sailors who are going down for their final count (THAT is a lot of swearing). The thing is, we do our very best to refrain from swearing, cursing, or embracing the foul vulgarity of explicit words in front of our children.

Now, I am not perfect (shocking, I know). One day my children will, more than likely, use that four-letter word we all hear and, dare I say, love to let loose. But I think that until you can grasp its meaning, and the proper time and place to use words of that nature, you shouldn't be expressing them.

We use these words to elucidate our feelings or thoughts, to accentuate a point. Sometimes they are just used. However, I don't believe a person who swears is able to be consistently cautious. We all slip up. I am a slipper-upper.

What's weird about it is that when the kids are away, we go way over the top. Now, I'm not a partier, and I don't get away from my babies very often, but when I do, I cuss! Every other word is an expletive. We have a helluva time hootin' and cursing.

And the funny thing is, I think I do it to feel like an adult. I know that may sound childish, but if I can say whatever the 'bleep' I want without 'getting into trouble,' then I am in charge, right? Seems like solid kid logic to me. See, I learn from them even when they are not with me.

I can go without, but if I am with my friends, I am going to cut loose and let those F-Bombs fly. Oh fly, F-Bombs, fly. I honestly imagine golden capital letter Fs with angelic wings flitting out of my mouth every time I let one loose. It makes my grown-up gene giggle, too.

There. Now that I know you must think less of me and you will read the rest of this book looking down on it and me, I will get to it.

My 3-year-old is a terror. One moment he manifests as the most loveable little boy possible, and in the next he is just downright B.A.D. (Boldly Acting Disobedient)

One day he was illustrating this point to a T. He did something he was not supposed to do and had been throwing a tantrum on for over half an hour. He was told to stand in the corner for time out. He did not want to do that. Go figure.

After all the chasing and panting like a dog running after a car, I had had enough. I told him it was naptime, partially because I now needed a nap after the chase.

This command prompted another round of chasing. Here I am, running around the house like a mad woman who's been defeated by a 3-year-old. I mean I was mad, but you know the kind I am referring to. I am hurtling through his room, trying to puff my body out to cover all of his escape routes, and yet he dodges me every time

I trip on a Transformer and do the instinctive 'jump on one foot and hold the other while trying not to fall or look like I am playing.' He laughs at me all the same.

It always makes matters worse when *they* laugh at *you*. As I pause to regain my composure, he dashes out of the room. Things aren't going very well for either of us at this point; he just hasn't realized the seriousness of his own situation yet.

Now it's hide-and-seek, while also playing chase. We like to get our money's worth in this house. He normally has a total of two spots he hides in. That's not the point, but it's so 'bleeping' cute!

As I pull the kid from beneath the table by the foot, he goes into full toddler meltdown, screaming like I am the monster from under his bed. For some reason running through my head is the song, "This is my hiney, this is my bum, look out Mommy, here I come" from a movie no kid should ever see, no doubt. Back to the story at foot.

I just know the cops will be showing up at my door any minute. At this point, I have hit my limit. My face is as hot as a fried egg... Yolk not included. I'm seeing red and this little rapscallion is just pushing me further than I want to go.

Out of nowhere I yell, "I'm going to spank your Ass!" As soon as the word is uttered, I become immediately ashamed. I just knew I had let it go too far. I barely react before he yells back at me, "Don't spankin' my ass, Mama!" while he grabs his buttocks with both hands. He looks up at me with those big brown sad eyes, full of both fear and expectation.

That was it. I burst into full on snorting laughter at this boy, who is literally holding his 'cheeks.' He looks at me like it's a trick for a second. Once he realizes he's not in trouble, he grins like nobody's business.

We sat on the floor laughing raucously and hugging so hard we fell over. God, I love this child! Needless to say, no spankings were delivered that day. And I did get my nap. That is the main point of the story, right?

Excuse me, but your age is showing

Last year I entered my third decade of life. No, I don't have difficulty saying it. Just thought it sounded better that way, don't you? No, really. Oh, joy.

I recently had the realization that my subconscious apparently wants me to embrace this whole 'growing old thing' a bit too much. Here's what I mean.

For a woman, getting older is not favored in our society. Aging is simply not looked upon kindly. It's an undeniable fact. So, how are we supposed to 'embrace it' when it repels a large percentage of the population? Seriously?

I mean, there are those occasional elegant older women in movies (usually old movies) who are able to capture the affections of the opposite sex while moving mountains with their wisdom and feminine power. They can carry their own and evidently, they are carrying it for the rest of us, too.

I live in the real world though, a world where youth and appearance play a much larger role in our ability to captivate. Well, at least in certain respects. Getting older and embracing aging has been difficult. Now, I know I am not a 90-year-old woman, but I am no longer 'Forever 21' and now that the decade of 2's has left me forever, well, it's harsh.

I guess my mind is playing a joke on me. It has decided that I am going to start forgetting everything I can. When I finally do remember, it will be exactly one day late. I hate being late.

My memory is leaving me; like that first gray hair leaves an indelible mark on your mortality *and* your vanity. I have resorted to notes in a desperate way.

I am talking a plethora of post-its, dry erase boards, chalkboards, calendars, and phone reminders. Notepads are climbing out of my purse in a desperate attempt to be seen. Paper is breeding and it has my handwriting (allegedly) all over it.

If I had any more alarms going off on my phone, a stranger might think someone was breaking into me, to steal a top-secret recipe.

First sign of aging: Begin to lose your mind, just enough to question if you are losing your mind.

Well played, crazy Susie, well-played.

The other day I had to go visit my mother-in-law. She had been working on threading a needle for some time and asked me if I could assist. I, of course, said it would be no problem. Well, let's just say I lied.

I take both the thick glaringly crimson thread and metallic silver needle in my hand. First, I make sure the end of the string isn't frayed so that I can thread it easily. Everything looks good so I get to work. Easy peasy. Poke, no. Poke again, uh-uh. One more time, I drop the needle. Great.

Second sign of aging: Lose touch with my motor skills (or losing my touch, touching things).

Now I am on my knees groping for the needle like a newly blind woman. I realized that this is a mission that requires my full attention. Hands are rubbing carpet in the most inappropriate of ways. I'm lying on the floor caressing the carpet with my face, sniffing, feeling, and I catch myself before trying to taste where this needle is nestled.

This carpet is like quicksand. No one ever talks about looking for a needle in quicksand. Quicksand trumps Haystack, take my word for it.

I'm still patting down the ravenous rug that swallowed my needle whole. Believe me, I'm giving it all I've got, doing my best not to poke myself, because I if I bleed out, then I won't be able to find the blood-red thread I am *still* choking, as it awaits its eventual passage through the eye of the needle.

Hmmm. Good quality rug. Very plush, wait, I almost forgot what I was doing. Breathe, grope, pray, aha! I finally find the needle.

We both stand there, look at each other for a second and silently acknowledge the humor *and* the annoyance of the situation. Finally, I thread the needle and cautiously hand it to her as though it is the last threaded needle in all of existence. Don't drop it. Do not drop it. We can't call for backup.

I know one thing. She won't be asking me to do that again anytime soon, nor do I plan on threading any needles for myself either! I surrender to using one of those little wire threader thingys.

Why would anyone be so foolish as to attempt a feat like this without it? And I don't consider it a concession to aging. I like to think of it as gaining wisdom.

Third sign of aging: Eyesight begins to diminish. Hooray. At least I'm getting something right.

I gathered the kids and headed out the other day. I now triple check the back seats to make sure I have all the kids I am suppose to have. I haven't forgotten one yet, but I just have this feeling...

I am not one to mess with CD's and such while driving. That takes a level of daring coordination I no longer have. See the above needle section if you don't believe me. (This may well be another sign of aging, but I am not going to admit it. Haven't I admitted to enough already? Geeze.)

I begin perusing the stations since I can do that without removing my hands from their 10 and 2 designated positions. I remember the days when I was young and headstrong and drove with only one hand on the wheel. What a rebel I was.

Nothing sounds interesting. I normally listen to classic rock to shield the kids from the influence of the 'inspirational' lyrics of today's pop music. But I'm sooooo tired of hearing what sounds like the same three songs over and over. You would think those classical rock stars would have produced more songs in all those decades.

I give in to a talk show that catches my ear. My memory takes me back to my teenage years, sitting in the backseat of my grandparents' Town Car, and being subjected to the endless blather of News Radio. It was torture to a teenager. I can still recall doing my best to pretend I couldn't hear. It seems like it was only yesterday that I swore I would never listen to that old people drivel again.

Then it hits me...I've been driving for 30 minutes half-listening *and talking* to talk radio! I've actually been muttering aloud as I agree and disagree.

I find myself asking my 3-year-old his opinion. He yells, "truck" and we both know that I am right. I am so engrossed in this debate, that when they go to a commercial break I feel a bit anxious with suspense. They return with a station ID. The station that has me so absorbed is NPR.

Whoa, when did I start listening to NPR? Not only that, but who programmed it into my pre-selected stations?

I have nothing against NPR, but I think I instantly aged 20 years (mainly from shock) when I heard those letters. My blood pressure shot up when the voice on the radio announced that I was in her territory.

I realized that I don't know half of today's pop music nor do I care for it. I long ago lost track of all the 'young artists' that are coming out. Bieber's beliebers, and the twerking jerkies, and Dear Lord, have I hit the era of 'who is that and what are they wearing?' Is that my youth I hear fading away in the distance?

I am sitting here listening to NPR and I am actually engaged in the content! I have officially not only become an adult but one who is both politically inclined and pooped on pop. Help. Me.

<u>Fourth sign of aging</u>: Becoming my grandparents.

What is this thing that is happening? My mind must be playing an ongoing practical joke on me. I don't have the heart to tell it to stop. Maybe I am just being a coward in some ways.

I just know that the 20-year-old me would slap me in the face and laugh (if the space-time continuum wouldn't collapse in on itself, were that to ever happen).

Let's recap my current aging predicament. I stay in every weekend because of the kids. Let's be honest, even if I didn't have the kids I don't know why I would be out on a weeknight or weekend for that matter. Perhaps, if I needed to go out and get some milk so I could warm it and drink it to help me get to sleep? Of course, had I made that late night run, I would be looking at the teenagers thinking that these 'hoodlums' need to be at home. It's 8:00, too late for anyone to be out. Wow. Welcome home old woman.

All I want to do is plant some Rhododendrons and read a good book. Maybe I'll take a nice sitz bath, whatever that is. I could crochet if I were able to see the yarn; of course I could buy some of those lovely bi-focals and get one of those lights that replicates sunlight with the magnifying bar enabling me to see virtually anything! Then I could sit peacefully and knit one, pearl two to my little heart's desire and until it exploded with glee. Parties and bars are for those young whippersnappers.

I am afraid that I am going to order myself a walker and start using it so I don't break my hip. It's just a precautionary purchase, but a good investment I'm sure. Someone needs to stage an intervention for me.

But really, there is nothing wrong with growing older. It's still growing, right?

Being a parent has opened my eyes, heart, and mind to a hidden world all around me. My children have led me to find passions I never knew I had. My love and need to protect them isn't only about them, it is an ever expanding desire to care for any child that needs more than what the world is providing them.

I want to enjoy my thirties. I want to find a new, extraordinary piece of myself as a 30-something and embrace this new chapter of my life with a fervor that my younger self could only dream of.

It's just that I think I may have jumped ahead a few decades already. Is there a reverse button or sequence somewhere? I will need someone to show me how it works, because this technology stuff is beyond me.

It's the End of the World Yet Again

I love philosophy. The Allegory of the Cave is one of my favorites. I love the idea that our perceptions create our reality. There must be some truth to this because I once perceived myself as Snow White. Now, my reality is one of being surrounded by miniature people. I mean constantly surrounded. Every minute, of every hour of my day is crammed with small humans. Gone are the days of philosophical debates and adult conversation.

There is no silent shower. There can never be a sneaky snack. Beds are no longer restorative safe havens. Hide and seek has become found and run. And they don't even bother to help with chores.

I am a child magnet from rise until fall. That's their rise, *in the wee hours of the morning*, and my fall in *the wee hours of the morning* exhaustedly into bed-- if I'm lucky.

Adult interactions are so much of a sought after treasure. I feel like a pirate without a compass clenching an age worn map. When I find them, I get lost in these rare moments of yesteryear. Lost and found. See what I did there?

My world is now so kid-centric that when conversing with adults, I feel like I forget how to actually be one. I have ample opportunities to stand up like a grown-up, but more times than not

I simply revert to being a child myself. What's up with that?

When home alone, (w/o adults of course. I made it clear that I am NEVER actually alone) I often engage in conversations with myself like questioning the existence of the television remote. Or I have at least one heated discussion per day over the health benefits of green foods. I do mean green foods too, not organic or vegan, but foods that are the color Green. If I am lucky, I might permit myself to listen as I divulge my insights on the validity of robotic noises and the legitimacy of their Anthropomorphism.

My life is filled with interminable conversations over the necessity of clothing and the moral implications of not wearing said clothes. I am an ever-flowing fountain of intellect and...Hang on; he lost his pants....again.

I can't tell you how many arguments I have had with a 3-year-old. I mean, I pick up a toy and refer to it, as a she, and he will not relent until I know I am as inaccurate as a broken clock. He will not tolerate me being wrong. He's worse than I am, and I'm a woman!

Don't even get me started on my responses to his child gibberish. If I don't respond correctly, I will be ordered into the adult version of 'time out.' The look in the eyes of this kid is just out of this world like he is Master of his own universe. It's as if his eyes silently scream, "Mom, you are really in trouble and I'm going to look at you like this until you realize just how lucky you are that I am unable to actually do anything but look at you like this." Welcome to my reality.

Just a friendly reminder: Kids live what they learn. I know it's a mind bender, but just think about it.

Here I am trying to let him know that it's time for bed and he is crying.

He's not crying because it's bedtime, though. He is crying because he is beyond tired. Does he want to go to bed? No. That would be absurd. He wants to stay up and watch a movie. No movie, Mommy? Well then, he wants to go to the library at 9:00 at night. We can't go to the library? You are a dictator, Mommy. I may not know what a dictator is, but I know that you most definitely are one.

He cries and looks at me with those big puppy dog eyes (the ones you see in those velvet paintings). Me thinks he thinks that I am so fueled by my/his emotions that I am unable of going against them. He climbs into my lap and plays with my hair in an effort to put me in a hypnotic state so I will be able to endure his continued cry and stop complaining about the situation.

He's exhausted, but he is fighting it. This kid will resist surrendering to sleep to the end. Then I'll eventually find him in a bathroom doorway or just outside the family room passed out in a heap like a drunken sailor. Or, like his batteries ran out.

Then what do I do? Oh, you know. I just blow a raspberry at the sleeping mini man to let him know that I was right. I did what? Yes, yes, I did and I'm not ashamed. Ok, maybe just a little shame here but he's asleep so I won. Then it's the old carry him to bed and sneak out hoping he doesn't wake and realize what's going down. Which just happens to be him.

Sooo, what's on the agenda for tomorrow night? Hang on, let me get my calendar. Ok tomorrow it looks like...oh here it is. I have scheduled a re-run of Bedtime with the Reeces. Repeat. Repeat. Moms just love to repeat.

Tonight I had a darling child with tears of sheer injustice streaming down his cute cheeks. I broke his heart by subjecting him to the *horror that is his bed!* His world ended and, in a moment of weakness, it made me tempted to give in. But I didn't, because dictators must never show weakness. Haven't your kids taught you that yet?

Tomorrow his world will rise anew and be filled with curiosity, laughter, and joy. Tomorrow night it will all once more be evaporated by the evil Momusa, whose snake hair transforms him into an unwilling victim of an endless slumber. At least that's his perspective.

I may not be able to debate Kierkegaard or Plato very often, but I sure can dish about the reality of sleep deprivation and the inevitable collapse of a 3-year old into a much needed hibernation. It's all relative anyhow. Or so I've been told.

The Sum of All Kids

My three remarkably unique children forced me (sometimes literally) to adapt to each of their needs--through this they taught me patience and understanding. Children make us better people by teaching us with everything they do. They create moments that turn into memories that will outlive the millions of photos you accumulate in their lifetime. (Fancy yourself a photographer? Hey, me too! Ooops, back to the conclusion.)

My trio of trouble has pushed me to be more of a person than I could have ever been on my own. Because of my kids, I've seen life in all its vibrancy, through splattered glasses, I've had kooky kitchen adventures, and I've never appreciated sleep more than I do now. I have learned (sometimes slowly, but I learned) that although children may not pay rent, they do pay us with their own treasure (rocks, snails, frogs, wildflowers that make you sneeze and all). They are a well full of untold riches, that will fill you when you feel empty.

I have gone from being terrified while struggling to install a car seat to understanding that I will survive---they've grown my confidence. They've shown me that I will figure it out, and that it's okay not to have all the answers all the time--they've taught me humility and that perfection is merely a mirage.

Parenting is a learning experience. Many parents practice 'Helicopter,' 'Free-Range,' 'Attachment' parenting, or a Hodge-Podge (that's my term and I'm sticking to it) of those and more. We choose what works best for *our* familial units.

I am but a Mom-losopher; a Mother who has pondered endlessly over the mind's, hearts, and souls that make up my parenting-offspring dynamic. Immense wisdom is found within the relationship I share with the gems I call my children. Let me tell you a secret my dears, you are, too, because your children are a never-ending source of learning.

Mom Prob: Once you have kids, you're like a set.

The set has less value if it is not complete.

All children learn, love, and live differently, and we all began as children. Hey, some of us have never grown up. You know who, the fun ones. Did you learn something there?

Every experience is a first for a child. We are all experiencing aspects of this life for the very first time. It's up to us to choose to remember how to see them through the eyes of a child.

Kids will test you every day and then, when you are at your breaking point, they will pull you into the very edge of their world. Opening your eyes to a world of wonder, a world of magic and of mystery. In that brief moment you can relive breathtaking emotions that once filled you as a tiny human. Theirs is a world where everyone and everything is special. Our children are capable of giving us the greatest gift. All we have to do is allow ourselves to see it when it happens.

Children need, and they need a lot, more than you can imagine and less than they think they do. But not necessarily as much as we impose upon them. We create needs that aren't vital to their survival or happiness.

'Keeping up with Jones,' having the latest iPad, Xbox, laptop, music downloads are keeping our kids from being kids. How much can one child handle before s/he is no longer a child? They learn through repetition, and over time, their memories adapt and retain that 'new' information until it's a part of who they are and will be. You have to ask yourself, what your child will be if that repetition is a video game?

We as parents need to be vigilant and not allow the insatiable desires and obsession with things to take priority in our lives. We simply need to understand their most basic needs: guidance, love, and providing them with a stable environment. They may not know what stable is, and they certainly don't contribute to it, but they definitely need it to become well-balanced people. When they grow up in a home filled with laughter, creativity, and most importantly, acceptance they can become more than well-balanced individuals, they can become anything they want.

Make memories. Find an old sheet so they can be a superhero you and they will never forget. Chuckle like a child at the covert cluster of cheerios. Roll on the floor with them until you stop thinking. Take a breath, slow down, and savor each bite of this course. Be fully present. Be there while *they* are there, because one day very soon your children won't be eating from the Kid's Menu.

Don't focus on the meals you ended up wearing, remember the ones you shared together, made together, ate together and then ate again together, as leftovers.

Be the parent that *YOU* were meant to be, and never forget who is really in control. The KIDS!

The End

Acknowledgements

To my Grunt, Ding-Ding, and Kiki, you have been and always will be my inspiration. Thank you for slapping me around and showing me that I could.

To my husband, Josh you so easily accepted the topsy-turvy world of writing and publishing. Without you, I would not have been able to create our children, or this book.

To my paternal grandparents for their amazing strength. You were my true north during our difficult storm. My love for you crosses the bounds of grandchild, you became my parents and I will forever love you.

To my mother-in-law, Cindy, thank you for being the only MIL in the Universe to make it into the Acknowledgements. You accepted me into your family with all your heart. I can never thank you enough for that and so much more.

To Ed and Lea Quinn, your love for my father has kept his love for me a constant throughout the years. And without the connection to your family I would not have been given the chance to pursue this book. Thank you for caring for me and for my father.

To Dan and Josh, without you we really would have been starving artists!

To Joan Quinn Eastman, my editor and dearest friend. You believed in me and my dreams when others did not and because of you I am making them a reality. We have held strong through the darkest days. You have been a surrogate mother, confidant, and guiding light. You inspired me to achieve more than the world thought I was capable of from the moment I first met you.

To Scott Anderson, our merry mentor, your words of wisdom and expert guidance kept us on the path to completion. Thank you for your generosity of spirit, for having faith in me and for joining the journey. You have been a thorough and delightful tour guide!

To my many friends who have shown me support and encouragement, thank you all! It has been a long road, but the scenery certainly gave me a lot to witness!

The warmest hearts are those where children live.

Three-enese Translation Guide

Bellwy – Belly

Ah-dan-der – Alexander

Dis – This

Sape – Safe

Ultra Magnus-tude – Magnitude- with a Transformer twist.

Meoark – The interpretative sound a cat would make if it could bark.

Ding Ding – Poorly chosen nickname.

Ahhhsome – Awesome

Roaaaarrrr – An exuberant roar.

Wahhhhh – A common term used when crying.

Otay (tay) – Okay

Goaoaehoaydesasdf – The coolest sound ever heard (at least for now.)

Wawee – Water

Spash – Splash

Nakey – Clothing Not Included

Prise - Surprise

Foods – Food times itself.

Woom – Room (not to be confused with Womb)

Awooooooo – The only sound all cars make.

Moob – Move

Ober – Over

Dank-coo – Thank you

Transformee – Transformer

Weeooo – Random noise.

Fiderman – Spiderman

Captch – Catch

Poo poo burp – Fart (Excuse me)

Scuse – Excuse

Cuz – Because

Wegi – Luigi (Brother to Mario)

Sabe – Save

Da – The

Marshmallow – Mushroom (Can also be marshmallow)

Oohohoohoh – Signifies excitement

Mmmmmhmmm – Mmmmmhmmm

Umhumhumum – Your guess is as good as mine.

Whatchoo – What are you? (Not asking what are you--this is the definition in question)

Dribe – Drive

Dere – There

Weeeeee – Squeal of joy.

Homeworks – Homework (Harder than it looks.)

Biggerest – Bigger and Biggest combined is still not as big as biggerest.

Duba – Love

MOM Probs Index

A quick reference for Moms and problems.
Author's Note: *When compiling this list it struck me that there are twice as many*
Mom Probs as there are MOMents...Just sayin'....

1. *Don't be a Yes Mom.*
2. *Sometimes you just need a dose of self-prescribed research.*
3. *Kids stink, literally. They smell from birth (although some find this smell appealing) until they realize they want to impress someone at which time they simply camouflage it. Boys smell worse than girls do. That's just another special perk of being a male.*
4. *You don't have enough batteries. Buy more.*
5. *Kids think they are funny. Sometimes they're right.*
6. *Exhaustion is a miserable side effect of being a parent.*
7. *If you don't know who did it, it was the kid.*
8. *Don't fuss over fashion. No matter what ensemble you choose they will put their designer stamp on it, as in spit-up or worse.*
9. *Kids cry. They communicate with that one the most. You don't have to cry to communicate with them, although sometimes you may want to.*
10. *If you hide it, they will come.*

11. The quiet game hardly ever works unless there is an incentive in sight and the game lasts no longer than their attention span.
12. Attention spans may vary in size.
13. Sometimes you may feel like you are losing your mind. Your children are behind this.
14. Invest in some Ginkgo Biloba and join the club. Now accepting new members.
15. All Parents worry. Lessen your worries by realizing that most are imagined.
16. You can talk to your imaginary worries if you want too. The rest of us do.
17. The television can be a babysitter during hard times.
18. Don't be surprised if the TV is chosen over you or any other activity for that matter.
19. You may think you have control. Don't kid yourself.
20. When the kids think it's the End of the World, stay calm. Kids are often wrong.
21. Everyone makes misteaks. (See what I mean.)
22. Potty training will happen. It is highly unlikely that you will have an 18-year old who still wears a diaper. Remember, I said 'highly unlikely.'
23. You will be judged. Don't expect to win anything though.
24. You don't have to be a real person if you don't want to.
25. You can be whatever you want to be, honey.
26. Savor that moment of relief when you find out your plans are cancelled.

27. Bubble baths
28. You will fight with them over eating vegetables. You will fight with them over eating dirt. One of you will end up eating one of these. I suggest you invest in winning.
29. If you always feel like you are forgetting something, it's probably because you are.
30. Never make up your mind about something until you actually experience it firsthand. This will keep you from making promises about what type of parent you will be before you really find out what type of parent you are.
31. Your body no longer belongs to you and you simply must accept it.
32. Climb on me like a jungle gym children. Do your worst.
33. Blaming yourself is an option, and a good one at that.
34. Kids have excellent memories, until you need them to find your keys.
35. There will always be more questions than there are answers unless you include silence.
36. Silence always constitutes a valid answer.
37. Kids are constantly getting 'hurt,' it comes with the territory.
38. There are times in a parent's life when you haven't seen another adult in so long that you find yourself being transported into another land. I call it the land of really short demanding people. Just go with it.
39. Zzzzzzzzzs.

40. They know they can get almost anything out of you and you have officially stopped trying to pretend otherwise.
41. Put your kids down so you can take a nap, too. Hush little kiddie. Mommy needs her rest!
42. Catch them if you can.
43. Don't worry. Parents never really know what's going on.
44. Sometimes there are just no answers.
45. There are days where you just have to_____.
46. When you're surrounded by little people you have no one who can help you reach the top shelf.
47. Children are dramatic. Prepare yourself to deal with miniature drama princes/princesses.
48. Having to push the 'car' cart at the grocery store to make your little one happy.
49. Being eyeballed by the 'normal' adults as you crash the 'car' cart into everything.
50. Sometimes you just have to pretend to be asleep.
51. Make snoring noises and don't peek because they are always watching.
52. Let go. You cannot do it all. Be what they need and let go of what's holding you back.
53. The days where nothing gets done and you're too tired to care.
54. Having a daughter and being girl clueless.
55. If you say they 'will' or they 'won't' they will do the complete opposite. Every. Time.

56. Getting a new accessory for the kids excites you more than it does them.
57. The box is always the best toy. In fact, just give them a box. It saves money and batteries.
58. The proliferation of Matchbox Cars and Legos is scary. (I see...legos.)
59. Your kids are officially embarrassed by you.
60. When did I become a Mom?
61. Using sneak attacks and bribery to give them the affection you know they want!
62. You are officially an adult. Just don't tell anyone I said that.
63. When you have to be an adult in a conversation and you just can't think of the word.
64. You don't have to compete with every other parent in the world.
65. Your kids won't care what Timmy down the road gets as long as they have you in their life. Besides who is this Timmy you speak of?
66. Everyone has parenting advice. It won't always apply to you and your family. Take what does and make it your own, then throw the rest out except for this book. This book is vital to your parental survival.
67. When reading, it's ok to make up words but you can't skip words. They know.
68. Use your camera. Often. You will need evidence when they are older.
69. Keep an extra set of clothes for everyone in the car especially when they're young.

70. You are going to doubt yourself, but if you are doing it right, I bet that your kids won't.
71. Teach your children. Enlighten them. Show them the beauty in the world and guard them against its dangers. YOU are their most important teacher.
72. Sometimes life can be boring, make it fun. Make sweeping a game.
73. Turn cleaning their rooms into a scavenger hunt. Create fun to fill those moments.
74. Realizing that you are 'that Mom' over and over.
75. Your pockets are never empty and yet none of the items actually belong to you.
76. When they fall asleep while you're out and you feel like a people smuggler.
77. Those two seconds that your back was turned. I didn't realize we had strawberry syrup!
78. When you're just too tired to clean it so you throw it away.
79. The moment your voice became that of your parents.
80. Trying to convince your infant that the baby food is edible.
81. We're gonna need a bigger bed.
82. Meeting another Mom you must immediately run through the 'Mom-patibility Checklist.'
83. Needing alone time and then feeling lonely when you finally get it.
84. Wanting to co-sleep and halfway through the night realizing you have made a huge

mistake. How can someone so small force me out of my own bed?

85. When little fingers pry your eyes open in the morning. That's illegal with a capital E.

86. Listening to them state the obvious all day long. I made a mess, Mom! Thank you for your commentary.

87. When you find yourself talking to the wall. Blank stares for days.

88. You're never going to be done cleaning up after them. Accept it! Do it. Do it.

89. When they sleep in too late and you begin to panic over SIDS even though they are 10 years old.

90. When you have impressed yourself with how fabulous the kids look and then you realize you are wearing two different shoes.

91. Your child has been on a yogurt kick so you go and buy 10 tons. Once you give it to them, they've decided they no longer like yogurt. Now what? Yogurt bath anyone?

92. They view laughing as a sign of weakness.

93. Nothing is off limits in the eyes of a 12-month old. I mean, they poop their pants. What's up with that?

94. Feeling like you are a Guantanamo Guard when you have to take your kid in for shots.

95. Your child is going through a growth spurt and you never have enough food.

96. Looking for a daycare or babysitter and considering getting a background check, psych test, hiring a detective....

97. Fighting with your kids over drinking water because you never realized it was an option. The doctors only ever suggest juice or milk.
98. Having intimate knowledge of another human's bowel movements. Smells and all.
99. What to do with the extras? Diapers, baby food, etc.
100. Everything hurts. You're never the same after birth.
101. Wanting them to develop, but then when they do you wish they were still little...
102. Breastfeeding.
103. Figure out all of these products!!!
104. Need an assistant to test everything first.
105. Mom Lingo. What's up with that?
106. You're a first time parent and you have to figure all of this Stuff out on your own.

MOMents Index

Author's Note: We are fewer in numbers but we are twice as powerful.
It all evens out in the wash...If you ever get around to it.

1. When your kid uses one of your good behaviors.
2. When you know you've done something for which they are going to adore you.
3. When you've finally found something they like.
4. When you've been away from them for a bit and when you see them again, they somehow look so different.
5. The first time they smile or laugh at you. And, every time after that.
6. When they do something 'normal' and you think they are a genius.
7. The first time they say your name.
8. All of the firsts...
9. When they're sleeping.
10. When you have more than one kid and they have a 'getting along' moment.
11. Every time you look at old photos.
12. When they favor you over anyone else.
13. Birth, or at least afterwards when you finally meet.
14. The first time you get to play a prank on them.
15. Introducing them to your favorite shows, movies, music and they <u>love</u> them, too.
16. Anytime you outsmart them.

42566585R00126